Jean-Claude Racinet

Racinet explains Baucher

XENOPHON PRESS

Jean-Claude Racinet

Racinet

explains

Baucher

XENOPHON PRESS

Cleveland Heights, Ohio

Cover by Lynne Gerard. Illustrations labeled Fig. 1 through 20 are from the 12th edition of François Baucher's book **Méthode d'Équitation** of 1864. Other illustrations by author and Natalya Romanovskaya

Published by Xenophon Press, 1772 Middlehurst Road, Cleveland Heights, Ohio 44118-1648, U.S.A.

ISBN 0-933316-08-9

Printed in the United States of America on recycled paper.

Foreword

In 1992, Ivan I. Bezugloff, Jr., then the Editor of *DRESSAGE & CT* magazine, asked me to write a few articles on Baucher and his equitation. This was the origin of a series of thirteen essays, published from November 1992 through November 1993.

This series was received more than favorably by many readers of the magazine who, subsequently, frequently expressed the wish to see these essays put together and made available in the form of a book. The present work is my response to their desire.

Some editing, however, was inevitable. An article is a unit in itself, the readers have to understand it even if they have not read the previous one. Repetitions, hence, are the rule. These repetitions were suppressed as much as possible in this book. The titles of the chapters also do not always correspond to the titles of the articles as published in the magazine. Moreover, the text was reorganized, whenever necessary, to bring about more clarity.

Two *Appendixes* were added; the first one deals with the validity of Baucherism, in light of the last discoveries of "equine osteopathy," as exposed by Dr. Dominique Giniaux of France; the second is a translation of the very last part of the 12th edition of Baucher's **Méthode d'Équitation,** dealing with his second "manner." This text has probably never been translated into English, and is of utmost importance. The riders who will endeavor to apply by the letter the progression described by Baucher in this text will, to their surprise, probably accede to a new and higher level of equestrian knowledge.

Jean-Claude Racinet
Anderson, South Carolina

Bo, a Quarterhorse, after two years of training in the principles of Baucher's second "manner".
• Engagement of hindquarters is accruing to the elevation of the neck.
• The rider is "resting" on horseback. The horse is self-impulsed. The legs are totally inactive. They start the movement and come immediately to rest.
• "The elevation of the neck compounded with the 'ramener outré' gives and fixes the true head set which thenceforth will never ever be lost" (Faverot de Kerbrech).

Contents

Foreword   v

Chapter 1
François Baucher (1796-1873)   1

Chapter 2
Baucherism: Philosophy and Method   15

Chapter 3
Baucherism: The Procedure   29

Chapter 4
The "Effet d'Ensemble"   45

Chapter 5
The Second "Manner"
Hand without legs - Legs without hand   53

Chapter 6
The Second "Manner"
The lifting of the neck   71

Chapter 7

    Légèreté vs. Durchlässigkeit   89

Chapter 8

    Lifting the Withers   103

Chapter 9

    Baucher and the American Riding Tradition   119

Chapter 10

    Practical Baucherism   133

Chapter 11

    Baucherism and Competitive Dressage   145

Chapter 12

    How Does One Become a Baucherist   159

Chapter 13

    A Letter To Susan   177

Appendix 1

    Was Baucher Right?   193

Appendix 2

    Progression of the Training   201

Chapter 1

François Baucher (1796-1873)

The rapid and relatively recent development of dressage in the United States has confronted the American riding public with a problem of acquisition of knowledge, not only on a technical, but as well a cultural plane.

At first, all the references were most often German, since the Germans win, and one knows how convincing *victory* can be for the average American! Then came the awareness of a possible difference between *dressage* and *artistic riding*, that is, *precision* vs. *beauty*. But here again, the references remained in the German cultural camp, since "beauty" was embodied by the adorable Lipizzaner of the Spanish Riding School of Vienna, Austria. All the dearer to the American hearts as they had been saved from Soviet claws by an American war hero, General George Patton. (An episode which even the lay public knew about, since it had been celebrated by a famous movie.)

At this point two names could be cited principally as authorities in matters of "classical" riding: Steinbrecht on the one hand, as the author of **Gymnasium des Pferdes (The Gymnasium of the Horse)**, which is the equestrian bible of many a contemporary German rider. Alois Podhajsky on the other hand, (director of the Spanish Riding School of Vienna 1939-1964), as the author of **The Complete Training of Horse and Rider in the Principles of Classical Horseman-**

ship.

Then came the name of Baucher, as an enigmatic, intriguing, and almost always controversial note.

To many an American rider, Baucher came to be known mostly because of the repeated and stern warnings of the two above mentioned German, respectively Austrian, authors *against* his teachings.

In **The Complete Training of Horse and Rider in the Principles of Classical Horsemanship** Col. Podhajsky rejoices that the old German riding masters Max von Weyrother, Seeger, and Oyenhausen "were powerful enough to withstand the teachings of Baucher and establish their method so firmly that, later, Plinzner and Fillis (a follower of Baucher and author) could not influence the riding in this country."

Further he adds: "In 1913, Fillis died in Paris, as forgotten as his teacher Baucher," a statement which, in addition of being needlessly demeaning, is also untrue since neither Fillis nor Baucher were forgotten—Fillis' teaching was officially adopted by the US Cavalry School at Fort Riley, as it was by the Russian Imperial Cavalry School in St. Petersburg, where he was on the faculty at the turn of the century—and since Baucher was never the teacher of Fillis.

In his **Gymnasium des Pferdes** published posthumously in 1884, Steinbrecht concludes almost all his chapters by bitter attacks against Baucher's method. 31 years earlier, his uncle by marriage Seeger, then the most representative personality of the German riding establishment, had written a red hot anti-Baucherist pamphlet entitled "Serious warning to the German riders," wherein he condemned every bit of Baucher's method, calling him in conclusion "the grave digger of French horsemanship."

While the excesses of these attacks may well fit the psychology of the German riders of yesterday and today, they can't help arousing the curiosity of other equestrians, namely Americans. Too negative a publicity sometimes turns out to be counter-productive. So much so that recently, one after another, two books extremely favorable to Baucher and his "cause" were published in the English language. The first is **Dressage** by Lady Sylvia Loch (Trafalgar Square Publishing, North Pomfret, VT). The other is **François Baucher, The Man and His Method,** by Hilda Nelson (J.A. Allen & Co. Ltd., London, England).

These two books will be a good source of information for the American riders about François Baucher; the second in particular, since it is devoted in its entirety to the French Master.

So, who was François Baucher?

François Baucher was born in Versailles near Paris on June 16, 1796. 29 year old General Napoleon Bonaparte's "Coup d'Etat" was to take place on December 2, 1798, so the childhood and youth of Baucher was to unfold during the Napoleonic era, which the French call the "First Empire."

At age 14, François Baucher was brought to Italy by an uncle who was managing in Milan the stables of Camille Borghèse, Prince of Sulmone, and husband of Pauline Bonaparte, a sister of Napoleon. Four years later, at the fall of Napoleon, Baucher came back to France. He worked for a short time in the stables of the Duke of Berry in Versailles, then decided to work for himself and by 1820 settled in Normandy where he managed first one, then two riding establishments, in Le Havre and Rouen.

Baucher evinced outstanding qualities as a rider, trainer, and riding teacher. Yet he deplored that the way horsemanship was taught at the time was unclear, vague, and futile, and he set out to create his own system which, he hoped, would be based on rationality and "scientific" observations.

His intellectual endeavor reminisces much of René Descartes', the famed French philosopher of the 17th century. Descartes' tool to investigate the field of philosophy was the *"doute systèmatique,"* or *"systematic doubt,"* by which he would eliminate all which could not be proven beyond any doubt, seeking some primordial truth on which he would base his *"reconstruction"* of the whole edifice. What he found out as an irrecusable postulate was the famous *cogito ergo sum, "I think, therefore I am."*

In a similar way, discarding systematically the old theories inasmuch as they did not satisfy his need for rationality, Baucher discovered that the sources of the resistance of a horse lay in the wrong division of his mass on the ground, added to the poor mastery, by the rider, of his forces, which he called *"instinctive."*

The stiffness, the contraction of the forehand — neck, poll, and jaw — was to Baucher's eyes what a horse uses in order to oppose his rider's attempts at establishing a better division of his mass, and/or at curbing his *"instinctive"* forces. These contractions increase as the movement creates more momentum.

Hence the proper education of a horse should start at a halt and from the ground by a set of flexions of the jaws, poll, and neck, added to some suppling exercises of the shoulders, haunches, and hindquarters.

Then the same flexions should be made on horseback at a halt.

Having in this way worked a horse *"part by part,"* Baucher would undertake the *"reunion"* of the horse through an exercise he called *"effet d'ensemble,"* which is sometimes translated, poorly in my opinion, by *"coordinated effect;"* Fillis in **Breaking and Riding** calls it *"general effect,"* which is fairly good. *"Comprehensive effect"* would still have been preferable, since the *"effet d'ensemble"* is an effect upon the whole of the horse, as opposed to the partial flexions which have preceded and prepared it. So I will, in these lines, simply use the French term *"effet d'ensemble."*

The *effet d'ensemble*, which will be described in a more detailed way later on, consists in applying simultaneously a progressive action of the legs and a corresponding resistance of the hand, in order to bring the horse to shorten his base of support, hence, collect himself. The *effet d'ensemble* is first practiced at a halt, then in motion, but at slow paces.

The horse being made absolutely light in his front end through the direct flexions of the jaw (the head is vertical, the horse chomps his bit, and the reins are practically looped), and progressively accustomed to working on a shorter base of support through the *effet d'ensemble*, is then under the absolute dominance of his rider. He is ready for whatever the rider will please to order him.

The advantage, for Baucher, of this very analytic, very progressive method is that much time is saved. By going slowly, by working first in place, then progressively at slow gaits, by thoroughly suppling the horse part by part, one goes fast as a matter of fact. How fast? Baucher would pretend (and as we will see, would sometimes prove in the facts) that he could bring any horse—regardless of his conformation deficiencies—to piaffe, passage, and flying changes of lead at every stride (an air which he is the inventor of), in. . .two months and a half! (We will, of course, discuss this point further on in these lines.)

Let's now return to Baucher's life, after this quick overview of his philosophy, which was certainly not out of place, as it will help the reader to understand the personage and his career.

In 1833, Baucher had his first book, **Dictionnaire raisonné d'équitation** (A Rational Dictionary of Horsemanship) published. All his method—which was to undergo many transformations in the course of his life—was already in it. It was, after the words of General Decarpentry (a leading authority in matters of French horsemanship), "a revolutionary manifesto."

This however did little to make Baucher and his method known to the equestrian public at large, since he was exerting his profession in the province, far from Paris (by the standards of the time).

So in 1834 Baucher set out for Paris, where he hoped his talent would find more exposure. And this didn't fail to happen. In 1837 he was hired with his horses (*Partisan*, *Buridan*, *Neptune*, and *Capitaine*) by Laurent Franconi, who was owning and managing the "Cirque des Champs Elysées."[1] He immediately became the idol of the lay public, and an object of controversy for the more educated riding elite, since his program was far from conventional. It included canter flying changes of lead at every stride (a novelty for the time, and, for the majority of the old fashioned equerries, a stunt devoid of any interest and any future), canter pirouettes on three legs, pirouettes at a piaffe whose cadence the rider would modulate at will, passage backwards, canter backwards, etc...

France's equestrian "who's who" immediately split in two camps: those who were for Baucher (most of the time with an ardent admiration), and the enemies (most of the time vehement, sarcastic, or appalled). The quarrel took an even more general cultural dimension as it soon involved prominent personalities of the world of literature, art, music, theater, etc...up to the Royal Court itself! (France at that time was a constitutional Monarchy.) This aspect is amply treated in the two books I have mentioned at the beginning of the present chapter.

1842 was a most important year in Baucher's career, for three reasons.

First and foremost, it was the year his book **Méthode d'équitation basée sur de nouveaux principes** (Method of Horsemanship Based on New Principles) was published. Heretofore, with the exception of **Dictionaire raisonné d'équitation** (1833), Baucher had only produced minor works, whose style was sometimes clumsy (**Dialogues sur l'équitation**, 1834; **Résumé complet des principes d'équitation**, 1837; **Passe-temps équestres**, 1840).

This new book met with an immediate success; three reprints in 1842, one in 1843, two in 1844, two in 1846, etc... Unfortunately, some awkwardness in the wording of his principles, added to some conceit, at times, as concerns his position vis-à-vis the old system of horsemanship, triggered off a violent reaction with many a professional, who mustered under the tutelage of Comte d'Aure. A bitter polemic ensued.

Secondly, 1842 is the year when Baucher's prowess with *Géricault* took place. *Géricault* was a three-year-old Thoroughbred stallion who was bucking all his riders off. His owner, the Englishman Lord Seymour, had let it be known that he would give the horse to anyone who could without falling tour on his back the "Bois de Boulogne," a park near Paris. A representative of the "anti-Baucherist camp", Vicomte de Tournon had tried and failed. Comte de Lancosme-Bresves, a recent convert to Baucher, had succeeded, albeit by a trick, since he had had himself surrounded by a group of friends on horseback during the whole trip, so closely that *Géricault* hadn't had much chance to fight.

But right or wrong, he had won the bet and Lord Seymour gave him the horse, which he in turn gave to Baucher, as an homage. Whereupon Baucher declared that he would show *Géricault* at the circus *within a month.*

27 days later, in the light of the gas chandeliers, amid the brouhaha of the crowd and the hubbub of the band, a calm and disciplined *Géricault* performed a program which included lateral work, canter pirouettes, single flying changes of lead, and a magnificent, slow, majestic rein back by which he went out of the ring.

Every one with a name in Paris had made a point to attend, supporters as well as enemies. Among others, the Duke of Orléans, son of the King and high commander of the Army, as well as Lt. General Oudinot, former commanding officer of the Cavalry School of Saumur and presently aide-de-camp to the Duke.

These two personalities were very supportive of Baucher and — third important happening in the year 1842 — it was then decided that his method would be experimented in the Army. For Baucher, a dream come true.

To start with, Major de Novital, head of the "Cadre Noir" of the Cavalry School of Saumur, and Major Rousselet, the most prestigious equerry of this team, were summoned to Paris in order to meet Baucher and assess his work. Novital was enthused and immediately converted. Rousselet, although very appreciative, was more reserved. Baucher had given him one of his horses, *Capitaine,* to ride, and he felt disoriented. He was a very soft man, so he simply stated, as he dismounted, "Il est trop fin pour moi" ("this horse is too sharp for me").

Then about forty horses of the garrison of Paris were trained by their usual riders under the direction of Baucher. On April 3, after 26 lessons, at the rate of two short lessons a day, these horses were performing tight evolutions at a canter, individually or in groups, remaining perfectly "on the bit." Noted General Decarpentry in **Baucher et son Ecole** (p. 89): "Such a result was perhaps not unheard of in the best training performed in the old way, but it would have taken at least one year."

The third phase of the experiment featured a course for officers, captains, and lieutenants, so called instructor students. It lasted 39 days. Wrote the major who was supervising the whole: "Not all of the officers had come with the belief that they could be taught something. After about 25 lessons all without exception had understood the method and acknowledged the superiority of the principles of M. Baucher." (Decarpentry, op. cit., p. 92.)

At exactly the same time an experiment on a bigger scale was started in Lunéville, in the east of France, where two brigades of cavalry were stationed. It was conducted by Baucher's son, Henri, and was intended to be concluded after seven weeks by a great "carrousel" comprising three shows: one performed by officers, the second by noncommissioned officers, the third featuring two companies of cavalry: one formed with the best of the horses trained according to the old way, the other made of young horses with only a few weeks of training, but with Baucher's method exclusively.

The Duke of Orléans, supreme commander of the French Army, had given notice that he would preside over this carrousel on July 20th. On July 13th he died in a carriage accident. The experiment was put on standby, and the triumphal carrousel did not take place. Baucher was losing his protector and his best chance. . .

The Duke of Orléans was replaced as the head of the Army by his brother Duke of Nemours, a student of d'Aure, the leader of the anti-Baucherists, and well decided in this matter, as in any other, to disagree with all that his brother had done.

In spite of all the positive, and sometimes enthusiastic, reports written by all the officers who had been in charge of monitoring the experiments, Duke of Nemours was firmly decided not to let Baucher's method be accepted by the Army. Said he: "Je ne veux pas d'une méthode qui prend sur l'impulsion." ("I do not want a method which restrains impulsion.") The German riding Master Seeger, in 1853, will use this quote as an epigraph for his vitriolic anti-Baucherist pamphlet **Serious Warning to the German Riders.**

A last experiment, which had been scheduled before the Duke of Orléans' death, took place in the Cavalry School at Saumur in February 1843. Although it met with the habitual success (the ad-hoc committee was "for," as were 67 out of 72 auditors), it was rudely curtailed after six weeks. Baucher was given his leave, his method was forbidden in the school, "with the exception of the training of young horses," a rather unexpected statement. (Nowadays, one would deem young horses less amenable to Baucherism.)

Although politics had prevailed over technical common sense, the method would not completely loose ground in the Army, since nothing or nobody could prevent the officers from training *their own horses* according to the method of François Baucher. And he would continue to teach, individually, innumerable officers, as well as civilians. . .

Embittered, but undaunted, Baucher set out to tour with the *Dejean Circus*[1] the principal capitals of Europe, meeting with great success. In Berlin, in particular, he at first aroused so much enthusiasm that the local riding professionals took offense and, led by Seeger, responded with such a violent verbal artillery barrage that it would forever kill Baucher's future in the German countries.

Back in Paris, on an afternoon of March 1855, as he was working a young mare in hand inside the circus ring, a huge gas chandelier came down from the ceiling and fell on Baucher. He barely escaped death, but was so hurt that he could not ride in public any longer.

Deprived of strength in his legs, Baucher undertook a revision of his method that would allow for this lacuna, and developed his "second manner" (*"deuxième manière"*), which in some respects looks almost like a denial of the first one.

In this second "manner" (this term being used to remain faithful to the French terminology), the "effet d'ensemble" is no longer the cornerstone of the edifice. It is now performed only occasionally to calm a turbulent horse, and implies mandatorily the use of the spur. Lateral flexions of the neck and poll are still enforced, but are limited to an "eighth" of flexion. The direct flexion of the poll (or "ramener"—classical head set with the poll the highest point, and the forehead vertical), is no longer looked for directly, but is the result of the general attitude of the horse; it comes about progressively as the "rassembler" (*collection*) perfects itself. In other words, the "ramener" is no longer a prerequisite for collection, but its result, its expression.

This direct flexion of the poll is prepared by flexions of the jaw *practiced with the head as high as possible*, the forehead in a horizontal position.

Lightness is now sought by the hand alone, by means of "half-halts" to oppose the "resistance of weight" and "vibrations" to oppose the "resistance of forces."

Last but not least, a new axiom is set forth: "Hand without legs, legs without hand."

As he heard of it, Major Gerhardt, an adept of the "first manner," exclaimed, "Then Baucher is no longer Baucher! " I will show in the following chapters that, quite the contrary, Baucher was becoming Baucher.

This axiom "hand without legs, legs without hand" appeared for the first time in 1864, with the 12th edition of the "method." That's quite a long time after the accident; but it is explained by the fact that the contract Baucher had with his publisher for all practical purposes prevented him from bringing any major changes in his text. Only by the 12th edition was he in a position to express himself more completely.

As a matter of fact, Baucherism was a "permanent creation," constantly perfected and constantly modified. The accident of 1855 acted as a mere catalyst and accelerated an evolution that was pointing toward the second "manner" as we know it from the texts of the 12th and 13th editions of the "method." A 14th edition, published posthumously, was edited jointly by Major Faverot de Kerbrech, one of Baucher's best students, and Baucher's son Henri.

The second "manner" was actively practiced by some officers in the French Army, and one can find its influence in the style of the French military dressage riders up to the 1950's.

Unfortunately, since Baucher did not show at the circus after 1855, this "reformed Baucherism" did not get the exposure it deserved.

On the other hand, in her otherwise very interesting work on Baucher, Hilda Nelson seems to have overlooked the seriousness, the consistency with which the second "manner" Baucherists stuck to the principle "hand without legs, legs without hand" up to the highest levels of their "dressages" (training). This is due to a regrettable error in the translation of a passage of General Faverot de Kerbrech's

Dressage methodique du Cheval de Selle d'après les derniers enseignments de Baucher recueillis par un de ses elèves (Methodic Training of the Horse After the Last Teachings of Baucher, Collected by One of His Students), 1891, which I will correct in due time.

This results in Hilda Nelson's book limiting Baucher too narrowly to his "first manner." I will therefore emphasize in the course of this book the "second manner."

Baucher died on March 14, 1873. His last words were reported by General (then Colonel) L'Hotte, who was at his bedside: "Then taking my hand and giving it the position of the hand of curb" ("main de bride"—the left hand—J-CR) he told me 'Remember well: always this'—and he immobilized my hand under the pressure of his— 'never that' and he drew my hand nearer my chest." (Translation J-C R.)

As we will establish in the next chapters, these words bear the greatest significance. Beyond the diversity of the proceedings, they stressed the deep unity of Baucher's doctrine. For only the "main fixe" ("fixed hand") allows one to get repeated yieldings of the lower jaw, which is at the core of the whole method.

---

[1] It must be remembered that in those days a circus was the only place where horsemen demonstrated their skills. In fact, the first known dressage competition was not held until 1873, when officers of the Austro-Hungarian Army came together in Pressburg (now Bratislava, capital of Slovak Republic), some 50 km down the Danube from Vienna, to compete.

Chapter 2

Baucherism:

Philosophy and Methods

Throughout his life, Baucher was a researcher. His discoveries were many, although most of them turned out to be "rediscoveries" of ancient proceedings which had somehow been lost track of. Flexions of the neck from the ground were already in use in the ancient Italian school. Concepts like the "ramener" (classical head set with poll the highest point and forehead vertical), the "demi-arrêt" (half-halt), the "descente de main" (total release of the grip on the reins), etc., of which he made abundant use, sometimes with a personal coloration, could all be found in La Guérinière's **École de Cavalerie** (1731). And so on...

Lieutenant Colonel Adolphe Gerhardt, an adept of the "first manner," who was an Alsatian and as such spoke both French and German, even found out that at least two German equerries, Christoff Jacob Liebens (**Reitbuch**, Leipzig, 1665) and Hünersdorf (**Deutsche Reitkunst**, Marburg, 1791) had already set up systems very similar to Baucher's. Baucher, of course, who didn't speak German, was totally unaware of this. He was a very honest man, not at all a plagiarist.

Baucher wanted to wage his battle (against the resistances of the horse) somewhat like Napoleon Bonaparte had won his victories: analyze carefully the enemy disposition, determine its weak point or its cornerstone, and then bring all his effort to bear on this very point and in so doing bring about an unconditional surrender.

This unconditional surrender he got from many horses, but probably not all, for a horse is not necessarily a *simple* system which relies on only *one* center. Quite the contrary; each horse is different, and the rules, even if reliable, must be adapted constantly.

Yet let's bear in mind that Baucher was a man of his time. He believed firmly in science, somewhat naively. For him, everything would be explained soon (horsemanship as much as everything else), and the explanation would have to be *simple*.

In his quest for the basic objective, the conquest of which all would proceed from, Baucher would have to waver quite a bit. He first believed he had found the answer in the "ramener." The verticality of the head would create balance, and balance would etc... The flexions of the jaw, rather crude at first, were only considered one among many supplings destined to prepare this "ramener."

Then, only by the fifth edition of his first method, came the "effet d'ensemble" (probably because, at least with his students, a still imperfect relaxation of the front end would result in a still imperfect balance). The "effet d'ensemble," as explained in the previous chapter, is a progressive and momentary opposition between hands and legs at a halt or at slow gaits.

Then he focused more and more on the direct and thorough flexion of the jaw, as we can assume from the works of his students, as well as from family documents of General Decarpentry, whose grandfather Eugene Caron was one of the early pupils of Baucher, and as confirmed also in a "dialogue between the horse and the jaw," figuring at the end of his 12th edition (which starts the "second manner"). (Says the jaw: "I conclude by saying that if the mellow mobility of the jaw endures at all the gaits, the horse's movements will be assured, precise and graceful.")

But in the meantime, he was probably looking toward a new and more refined "golden key," since the flexion of the jaw he obtained in his second "manner" on a very elevated neck with the head at first horizontal might not have been exactly in the same vein as what he obtained in his first "manner" on a systematically "depressed" neck.

General L'Hotte, who, as a lieutenant, took a few lessons from Baucher, and during the rest of Baucher's life took constant advice from him, noted in **Un Officier de Cavalerie** ("A Cavalry Officer," 1905) that "each new discovery tended momentarily to throw all the others in the shade."

All this could give Baucherism a somewhat variegated appearance if one does not take sufficient distance to judge it. What common measure can there be between the "ramener" *as an absolute prerequisite* in the early days and the same "ramener" as a (blessed) *result* of the second "manner"? Between the "effet d'ensemble" and "hand without legs, legs without hand?" Between the *constant, nay forceful,* use of the legs ("The rider, true, did not bear anything with the hands; but he was carrying the horse with his legs," L'Hotte) and the request for releases of hand *and legs* in the second "manner?" Between the systematic use of the "diagonal effect" (hand and leg diagonally opposed, Raabe) and its condemnation and replacement by the "lateral effect" (hand and leg on the same side, L'Hotte, Faverot de Kerbrech)?

None, of course. Yet Baucher did not alter a jot his philosophy during the whole course of his life. This deserves an explanation.

As concerns the function of locomotion (movement), a horse's anatomy presents two different sets of muscles. The first set assures the locomotion as such. But it could not work without the other, which keeps the "carcass" together and provides the necessary "fulcrums."

The goal of dressage, its "raison d'être," is the enhancement of the gaits of a horse. So to train a dressage horse, basically, is to perfect and fortify the second set of muscles, the "fulcrum," in order to allow it to give the other set its optimal chances of "expression."

The old—"classical"—system, as well as the contemporary FEI-adopted one, works this set #2 (the fulcrum) *indirectly* by putting to work system #1 (locomotion) in a series of exercises articulated in a carefully studied progression.

Constraint is not absent from this progression, since the horse has to find in himself the energy to respond to his rider's demands for perfection in the execution of each movement. For instance, La Guérinière (**École de Cavalerie**, p. 183, translation is mine) writes that the "Pas d'École" ("school walk" or collected walk) is of great aid "to help a horse endure the suffering and the fear of the violent lessons that one is obliged to give him in order to supple him and confirm him as he progresses in obedience to the hand and the legs."

The purpose of the progression is to carefully break down the global constraint, each new movement bringing in its share of acceptable constraint.

Hence the adoption of trot as a "mother gait;" trot displays more energy than walk but is more economical than canter. Hence the notion of "working" gaits, and one understands that the Germans have heretofore clung to this concept. Germany is basically a Protestant nation, and for her, Man, even in his pleasures, remains stricken by the Biblical curse and cannot avoid the necessity of "working."

Hence the title of Steinbrecht's **Das Gymnasium des Pferdes**. Lightness will, perhaps, blossom tomorrow as a reward. Today is a time for sweat. Ballet dancers can't help having big calves. The dressage horse should first be an athlete.

Baucherism, by contrast, tries to work set #2 *directly*. For Baucher, in the beginning of training, movement is an *enemy*, or at least a nuisance, something which unnecessarily complicates the rider's task and the horse's comprehension of what is being studied. In his second "manner" he will coin the expression "separation of force from movement," to stress the advantage of frequent and short periods of rest in the course of a working session.

With the "effet d'ensemble," he tries to realize the "balance of forces" (the propulsive and the retropropulsive) *at a halt* first. He will then introduce movement as with an eyedropper, drop by drop, always controlling with the utmost care the "side effects" it will not fail to have upon a balance so painstakingly obtained at halt.

One could think that when a horse is moving, he is less apt to resist his rider, since his base of support is continually evolving and deforming itself. Not so says Baucher; it is at a halt, his four legs anchored into the ground, that I am better off dividing up his weight. I shall say more; I will, at a halt, prevent the horse from moving even one of his limbs at his own will. This is one of the main goals of the "effet d'ensemble:"

Establish the total subservience of the horse.

Baucher's aim is to suppress any initiative on the part of the horse, to replace what he calls "instinctive" forces with "transmitted" ones. This awkward wording (for how can a rider "transmit" any forces to his mount?) did much disservice to Baucher, although he later tried to use more nuanced expressions such as "harmonized" ones, etc.

May I come up with "my" own wording? I would have said "replace instinctive forces with induced forces."

But Baucher was not much of a writer. This is why to understand him, one is sometimes better off resorting to his pupils' works, because Baucher was an outstanding teacher; his oral teachings were clear, logical, and devoid of contradictions.

Even though the "effet d'ensemble" was to lose its prominence in the second "manner," even though the release of hand ("descente de main") would be accompanied by a "release of legs" ("descente de jambes"), the aim of total subservience of the horse remained unaltered to the end. I will come back to this point later, but surprising as it may be, when framed between "the weight of the reins and the stroke of the boots," a horse is much more under his rider's dominance than when he is more or less "bearing" onto the bit.

Let us come now to this very careful progression which introduces the movement little by little without ever taking any chance of the horse expressing his "instinctive" forces. It afforded at least two big advantages as Baucher saw it.

First and foremost, the difficulty being "broken down," the horse would learn his task much more rapidly. Hence the adoption of walk as a "mother gait." One would be tempted to call it a "working gait," but the notion of "work" (with its physical connotation) is much less prevalent here than that of "study." Walk is the gait for studying.

Here again, Baucher is much less of a precursor than he imagines. The late René Bacharach (**Réponses équestres**, Caracole Publisher, Paris) quotes on this subject Imbotti de Beaumont ("The key of the [equestrian] science is to know how to work a horse at a walk," 1682), Dupaty de Clam ("Walk allows the horse to feel all the operations, to single them out; he is not distracted like in a trot...," 1769), and Mottin de La Balme ("Go slowly and for a long time in order to make it easier to position the horse and educate his memory in an easy gait...like that of a walk," 1773).

There is also the celebrated example of François de la Lubersac (1713-1767), Equerry at the Military School in Paris, who, reports General L'Hotte, "would ride his horses for eighteen months to two years, only at a walk; and when after this time he gave them to ride to his best students, these latter would have the surprise of finding them 'dressés' (trained) to all the gaits."

The other advantage offered to Baucher by the "eyedropper" introduction of movement into his progression is that it allows the rider to constantly keep his horse "enclosed." This is another obsession with Baucher. For him, a horse can give utterance to his "instinctive" (hence rebellious) forces only by opening his frame. When the horse is properly "enclosed," he thinks, his center of gravity and the "center of forces" coincide; the horse is in perfect balance and can do only what his rider allows.

"I lived in Berlin for several months; I saw the German riding put into practice in its entirety. I do not have the pretense of setting myself up as a censor; I shall simply say that the principles held in Prussia are diametrically opposed to mine. For instance, several officers who bear in their country some reputation as riders would tell me, 'We want our horses ahead of the hand.' 'And I,' I would answer, 'I want them behind the hand [bit] and ahead of the legs. Only with this condition will the animal be under the total dominance of his rider'...Because, I would tell them, a horse ahead of the hand is behind the legs, and then *he evades your actions with both ends*..."

(the italics are mine, as is the translation). [Baucher, **Complete Works**, edition 1864, footnote p. 108.]

But what is an "enclosed" horse if not a "collected" one? One therefore understands that Baucher wants collection *at once* and will never allow the horse to depart from at least a beginning of a collected attitude. This, of course, deprives him at the start of some of the possibilities of evolution with his horse. Baucher does not care; it is a deliberate choice.

Baucher would also state that "position precedes action," which reflects the same philosophy. In other words, never ask for any movement if the proper position has not been established beforehand. He even tried to elevate this idea to the rank of a law. The law would state that "movement is the result of action upon position."

This would mostly apply to canter work. To obtain a flying change, Baucher would simply revert his aids (hand and seat) in order to give his horse the position of the new canter (no specific demand with the legs; the legs only maintain the impulsion, that is, the action), and the new movement (the new canter) would automatically ensue.

That Baucher, through this technique, became the first rider to overcome the difficulties of the flying changes at every stride of canter, and that his disciples of the second "manner" would pass these flying changes at every stride *with the hand only*, certainly speaks in favor of this point of view!

The law has other fields of expression. If, for instance, we can bring the hind legs way under the body *and maintain them in this position* (which Baucher would obtain by the practice of "effet d'ensemble") regardless of the gait, we will make the horse come to a quick stop. Baucher would obtain spectacular "parades" almost exclusively *with the spurs*, the hand intervening in the end only *to confirm the position* so obtained.

If, from a trot, we can sit a horse on his haunches progressively while keeping the action, we will get a piaffe. If we sit the horse on the haunches as he trots, and we increase the action, we will get all the nuances of the extended trot, up to the "Spanish trot," if we increase the sitting on the haunches and the action together. And so on...

(It would be fascinating to pursue this inventory of the fields of application of the "law"—and we would probably find exceptions in some lateral movements—but that would carry us too far away.)

Another "hue" of the same color in the Baucherist philosophy is the constant seeking of "lightness" as *a prerequisite* to any movement.

What is lightness? It is the absence of resistances of weight and strength to the rider's hand and resistances of inertia to his legs. In other words, and to be very simple, if the rider, in order to obtain what he wants from his horse, has to afford *any* physical effort, the horse is not light.

Now, how can lightness, which manifests itself during the riding process, be considered a prerequisite? Here we enter the core, the sanctuary, of Baucherism. Baucher, in effect, *equates lightness,* lightness as a whole (as defined above), *with lightness of the mouth.* For Baucher, if the horse is light in his mouth, that is, if his lower jaw gives at the slightest indication of the reins, proof that it is *relaxed*, the horse is light altogether; the resistances will have disappeared, resistances of weight and strength, of course, *but also resistances to the legs.* When the lower jaw relaxes, the horse is in a "state of grace" which Baucher calls "balance."

This is the basic postulate of Baucher, his "cogito ergo sum" (see previous chapter).

The ancient school, of course, was fully aware that the suppleness and relaxation of the lower jaw always *accompanies* the overall lightness of the horse, as described above. Lightness of the jaw is the *indication* that balance has been realized.

The genius of Baucher is to have made from this *manifestation* a *prerequisite*. By cultivating the sign separately, but creating it out of its usual context, Baucher forces the *reality* which justifies the sign, to appear (if only for a very short time in the beginning). It is *symptomato-therapy*, a *feedback technique*.

Symptomato-therapy is a medical process which consists of blocking the symptoms when the cause cannot be attacked directly. Stiffness or tenseness of the jaw is a symptom. For Baucher, imbalance is the cause. If I can relax the jaw, some muscles which were unduly tense will have to relax; some others which were unduly idle will be put to work. The "balance of forces", that is, the equilibrium between the propulsive and the restraining forces, will be realized so that *only the minimum amount of force* necessary to the movement will be spent by the horse.

From here comes the unforgettable and unquestionable definition of "lightness" by General L'Hotte: "The inducement by the rider and the use by the horse of the only forces necessary to the envisioned movement." (**Questions Equestres**, p. 39, translation is mine.)

I have spoken of the "feedback" technique; this is how it works. Each time a horse is willing to relax his jaw under the pressure of the rider's rein(s), the logic of lightness puts to work the muscles of set #2 (which I mentioned at the beginning of this chapter), which bring to realization the "balance of forces." The repetition of these actions will progressively (and rather rapidly, in fact) *build a new horse* who will no longer need the help of the rider to maintain his balance.

This has a name: self-carriage.

This "postulate," by which overall lightness is equated with lightness of the jaw, was not obvious to Baucher at once. It seems to have emerged slowly, as the method progressed; I will explain how later on.

One even wonders whether Baucher has ever clearly formulated this postulate. Let us come back, for instance, to the footnote on page 108 in the 1864 edition of his **Complete Works** (which I mentioned above) in which Baucher explains to his German interlocutors that "if a horse is ahead of the hand, he is behind the legs." We have here the "negative" of the postulate. The logical development of these words could well be "and if a horse is behind the bit (understood: in hand), he is *ahead of the legs!*"

I am well aware that at this point of my exposé, I risk confusing my readers, since nowadays, the expression "behind the bit" also implies the notion of being behind the legs. This idea, which was introduced by Fillis, applies to the horse who drops his bit in disgust with a gaping but stiff mouth, so much so that he refuses to move forward; this, which may well have been a possibility for a horse worked according to Fillis' method, has nothing to do with the lightness of jaw as looked for by Baucher.

Besides, the expression "behind the bit" is quite ambiguous. On the one hand, it applies to a horse who is overbent, his head behind the vertical. On the other hand, it implies a notion of refusal of contact with the bit. Now, many horses in this "bison-like" position are, on the contrary, pretty much bearing on the bit. So cosmetically, they are "behind the bit" but in fact, they are "ahead of the bit."

To come back to my talk, the fact that I wanted to establish is that for Baucher a horse that becomes light to the hand becomes by the same token light to the legs. This can be verified every day.

To sum up this exposé of the philosophy of Baucher, we are in the presence of three notions which are absolutely specific to Baucherism and which underlie the whole system. The first idea is that balance must be established prior to the movement rather than expected from it. The second idea is that balance, as a "state of grace," *can be established at a halt* by means of "effet d'essemble" and/or direct flexion of the jaw. The third idea is that lightness of the jaw *entails overall lightness*.

Obviously, this last idea leaves us with a choice to make between the "effet d'ensemble" and the "direct flexion of the jaw" as a way to obtain balance prior to the movement, because lightness entails balance.

The confusion here, in Baucher's mind, is greater than one might think. In his seeking for "balance first," a balance which could be established at a halt, he first relied on the mere "ramener" (verticality of the head). This ramener was obtained by means of direct "flexion" of the jaw, but there is uncertainty about what this "flexion" represented, since we still haven't heard of the "mobility" of the jaw upon the rider's request, which will progressively become, as the doctrine evolves, the technique's "core."

By the 5th edition appears the "effet d'ensemble," which intends to "distribute the weight of the mass equally on the four legs and produce temporary immobility."

But if balance entails lightness, and if lightness entails mobility of the lower jaw, should not the "effet d'ensemble" lead to it as well? Still, Baucher did not, at first, claim this as a purpose of the "effet d'ensemble," and rightly so, because (and this is another instance of incoherence) the flexion of the jaw comes *before the "effet d'ensemble" in the progression.*

This strongly suggests that what Baucher would call "direct flexion of the jaw" in the beginning of his career was probably far from the delicacy and subtlety of the mobility of the jaw that he so praised in his 12th edition.

Be that as it may, it is clear that, as the method evolves, there is increasing redundance between "effet d'ensemble" and flexion of the lower jaw. After an intermediary period when the "effet d'ensemble," or at least an opposition of the spurs and the hand, will become the usual way to ask for the relaxation of the jaw (Raabe), the flexion of the jaw *obtained by the hand alone* ("second manner"), will progressively evict the "effect d'ensemble," relegate it to a minor role, and, with it, *drastically abate the role of the legs.* Parallelling the "descente de main" (release of hand), the "descente de jambes" (release of legs) will appear.

And the ultimate stage of this evolution will find its expression in the provocative title which the greatest Baucherist "second manner" student of all time, Beudant, will give his last book: **Main Sans Jambes** ("Hand Without Legs," 1943).

So we know now what Baucherism really is: the seeking of lightness—hence balance—through a constant relaxation of the lower jaw of the horse. And we can assess what distinguishes it drastically and *definitively* from the German riding of yesterday and today. Whereas the latter seeks to confirm the "appui" (leaning onto the bit), the former tries by all means to destroy it.

I will certainly develop this observation, but we must first further examine the procedures of Baucherism.

Chapter 3

Baucherism: The Procedures

The ancient school would work the horse as a whole, trusting Mother Nature on the selection of the specific muscles to be suppled or strengthened to meet the requirements of a given exercise. Baucher would supple the horse part by part by means of "flexions" which would apply to: 1) the jaw and neck, on foot and on horseback; 2) the shoulders, by rotations around the haunches, on foot (second "manner") and on horseback (first and second "manners"); 3) the haunches, by rotations around the shoulders, directly on horseback in the first "manner," on foot first in the second; and 4) the lumbar area, by the movement of "rein back." He would then reunite the whole with the "effet d'ensemble." Let's examine all this in detail.

Flexing of the Jaw and Neck

a) The *lateral flexion of the jaw*, on foot, with the reins of curb. The head is progressively turned to one side until it almost looks backwards (Fig. 1&2); by the end, the horse must "chomp his bit" *as proof of success of the operation.*

"Chomping the bit" is vague and may be misleading to those whose background is strictly limited to German horsemanship. The real flexion of the jaw goes far beyond any "munching" of the bit. It must induce the jaw "to yield by opening under pressure of the bit,

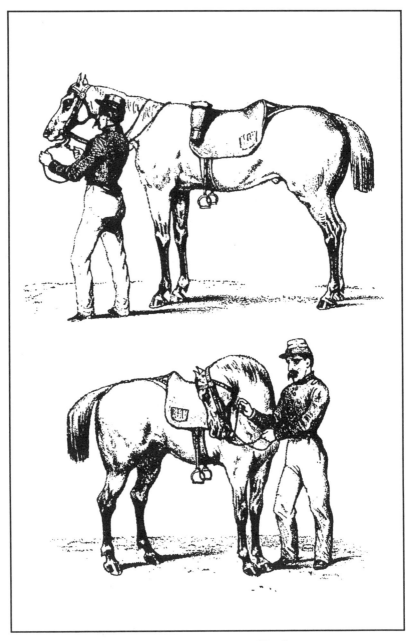

Top: Fig. 1 • *Bottom: Fig. 2*

whilst the tongue is mobilized up to its fixation under the poll, whose slackening is thence increased to furthermore facilitate the direct flexion" (i.e., the "ramener"). [General Decarpentry, **Baucher et son Ecole**, p. 51, translation is mine.]

Yet Baucher himself uses the verb "mâcher," which means "to chomp." "Le cheval, en *mâchant* son mors, constatera la mise en main...etc." ("The horse, by *chomping* the bit, will show his being in hand as well as his perfect submission.")

It is probable that Baucher did not ask more than a "munching" in the beginning, since flexion of the jaw alone, independent of any movement of the neck, was not his main preoccupation. Later, he realized that he had to relax the jaw *before suppling the neck*. He then focused more and more on the process of mobility of the jaw, which General L'Hotte described as a "mellow giving which may be only a light murmur" (**Questions Equestres**, p. 40).

General Faverot de Kerbrech gave of it a more elaborate description: "The mere 'half-tension' of one rein, or both, must bring about the mellow mobility of the lower jaw without the head's moving, without any noticeably apparent opening of the mouth; and the animal's tongue must then make one bit jingle over the other, which at times produces a silver-toned ringing" (**Dressage Méthodique du Cheval de Selle**, pp. 7-8).

This very refined process applies, of course, to the "direct" flexion of the jaw, that is, that which is done when the horse's neck is straight. It shows, however, that the relaxation looked for by the end of the "lateral" flexion of the jaw should not be limited to a mere "chomping" but should, on the contrary, be a rough draft of the more sophisticated direct flexion and at any rate include the up and down movement of the tongue and a "let go of the bit."

[31]

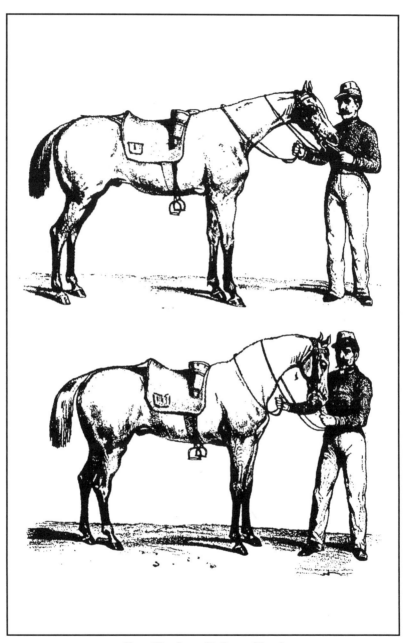

Top: Fig. 3 • Bottom: Fig. 4

Let us notice that "lateral flexion of the jaw" is not a very appropriate designation. As a matter of fact, it is more about a lateral flexion of the fore part of the neck than of flexion of the jaw properly speaking. Besides, this wording could make one suppose that the lower jaw is flexing laterally with respect to the general direction of the head, which, of course, would be a gross error.

b) The *suppling of the neck and direct flexion of the jaw*, on foot. The rider, facing the horse's head on one side, holds the reins of snaffle in one hand and the reins of curb in the other. He then pulls down the horse's head with the reins of snaffle as he in the meantime makes an opposition with the curb in order to bring about an opening and a yielding of the horse's jaw. The head should "yield of its own accord and by its own weight" (Fig. 3 & 4).

Two other manipulations may be done. In the first, after having crossed the two reins of snaffle under the horse's chin, the right rein in the left hand and vice versa, the rider will apply a steady and graduated pressure, up to the "surrendering" of the head (Fig. 5).

The other manipulation aims at suppling the mouth independently. One rein of snaffle is pulled forward, away from the horse, as the rein of curb on the same side is pulled backward. The pressure must be steady. The flexion is done not only when the horse opens his mouth (he doesn't have much choice) but when he relaxes it (Fig. 6).

c) The *lateral flexion of the neck*, on foot, with the reins of snaffle first, then with the reins of curb. The rider stands at the level of the horse's shoulders. The inside rein is passed over the neck, just before the withers, and comes in the inside hand of the rider. The other rein is held normally by the outside hand. Then the rider pulls progressively onto the inside rein as the other rein allows the movement by sliding gradually in the rider's hand. When the head is correctly turned inward, the heretofore "passive" rein re-establishes a contact in order to place the head in a vertical plane and to ask for relaxation of the jaw (Fig. 7 & 8).

d) The *direct flexion of the jaw and neck*, or "bringing in hand," on foot, only in the second "manner." The rider is in the same

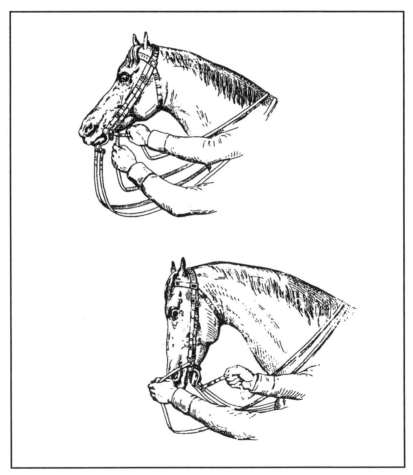

Top: Fig. 5 • Bottom: Fig. 6

[34]

Top: Fig. 7 • Bottom: Fig. 8

position as for the lateral flexions of neck, but he keeps the horse straight and uses reins of curb only. The jaw must yield first, bringing about flexion of the neck (Fig. 9). This flexion, in the second "manner", replaces the direct flexion of the first "manner" [see text under f)] where the bending of the neck precedes the yielding of the jaw.

e) The *lateral flexions of the neck from horseback*. They follow the same pattern as on foot, but here, the rider doesn't use any "fulcrum" on the horse's neck for the action of the inside rein. The outside rein, at first "passive," slides in the rider's hand; by the end of the flexion, it restores contact with the mouth to place the head in a vertical plane and to ask for relaxation of the jaw (Fig. 10 &11).

f) The *direct flexion of the head and neck*, or "ramener," done from horseback, first with the reins of snaffle, then curb. The rider takes the reins in the left hand, then sets the outer edge of his right

Fig. 9

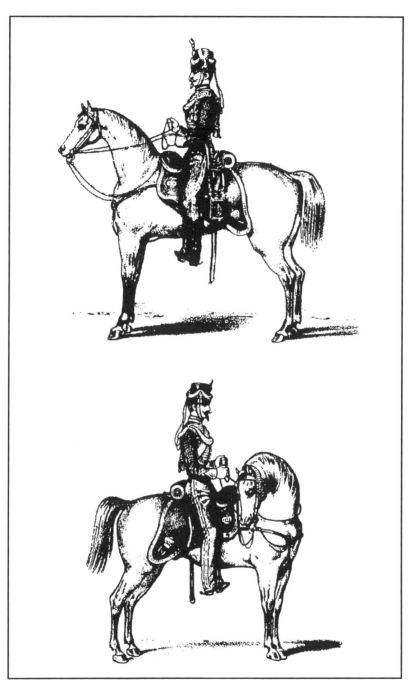

Top: Fig. 10 • Bottom: Fig. 11

hand on the reins in front of the left hand in order to establish a progressive pressure on the bit. The pressure matches carefully the resistance of the horse, since the latter should yield and not be forced (Fig. 12 & 13).

As concerns the final result of the flexion, Baucher states that, "the horse will have completely yielded to the action of the hand when his head is carried in a position perfectly perpendicular to the ground; from that time, the contraction will cease, which the animal will show, as in every other case, by *chomping his bit*" (italics are mine).

In the 12th edition, the whole paragraph I quoted above is replaced by this simple sentence: "The horse will have completely yielded to the action of the hand when *his jaw is mobile*" (italics are mine).

This difference in the wording ("mobility of the jaw" vs. "chomping the bit"), as well as the absence, in the 1864 edition, of any reference to the final position of the head, expresses well the evolution of Baucher toward his second "manner," in which the "ramener" is no longer a *prerequisite* but rather a *result*, as it proceeds from the mobility of the jaw.

Is this result immediate or progressive? Baucher doesn't tell. We will come back to this matter later on, as we shall study more particularly the second "manner."

g) The 12th edition also shows a *direct flexion of jaw* from the ground in a *very high position of the neck*, the head being horizontal.

It is very difficult, by reading this 12th edition, to know exactly what pertains to the second "manner" and what doesn't, since all the flexions of the first "manner" have been kept and they partially contradict the spirit of the second "manner." For instance, the flexion described in section b), which involves a depression of the neck, is in

Top: Fig. 12 • Bottom: Fig. 13

total opposition to the flexion of section g). Did g) suppress b), or are both flexions practiced together? We don't know. As a matter of fact, when the second "manner" developed, a total rewriting of the method would have been necessary, instead of the patchwork which the 12th edition is. The revising was visibly scamped, for lack of time certainly, and probably also because Baucher was reluctant to acknowledge the real dimension of the transformations he was bringing in.

In fact, in the second "manner," all the flexions are done in a *very high position of neck*, and the lateral flexions are less accentuated than before.

The flexions offer a perfect example of the evolutionary character of the method. They were done on a more and more elevated neck less and less laterally, and they aimed more and more at *mobility of the jaw* rather than its outright gaping. Their number changed; certain ones were added, others disappeared. Gerhardt, a student of the first "manner," even ended up dropping them completely, probably because mobility of the jaw can be directly obtained with most horses provided one has tact.

The flexions should be done *very slowly, very progressively, and very softly* in order to "invite" the horse into flexing. This is most important, since their aim is relaxation.

The outright bending of the neck in the lateral flexions, in the beginning of the method, would scandalize Baucher's critics. Baucher himself later brought more moderation into their conception. Nowadays, however, as equine osteopathy is beginning to develop (in Europe), we can realize that perhaps here again, Baucher's intuition was right. This flexion, indeed, by the elongation of the spine it provokes, can have the most beneficial effect on the whole structure of a horse; it serves as a basis for all the manipulations aimed at releasing lesions of the cervical vertebrae, most particularly the seventh, whose "locking" may be very detrimental to a horse's physical integrity.

Though the flexions imply the use of a double bridle, curb plus snaffle, they can be done on a horse mouthed with a simple snaffle. This just requires more patience from the rider. By 1840, that is, by the very beginning of Baucher's career and two years before the publishing of the **Method**, Maxime Gaussen would note in a preface to **Passe-Temps Equestres** that already the French Master trained "all his horses" (which is, perhaps, exaggerated) "with a simple snaffle."

This, anyway, belies completely the image of a forceful rider so complacently entertained by Baucher's enemies.

Turnings Around Haunches and Shoulders

These are started with the rein and the leg on the same side (left rein and leg to turn to the right and vice versa). Progressively, the horse is asked to perform these movements in a direct bending, that is, bent to the right if his haunches or shoulders are pushed to the right. In this case, the turning around the haunches becomes a classical "pirouette;" the turning around the shoulders becomes a "reversed pirouette." This latter movement is not acknowledged by the FEI.

To start the training of a young horse with these movements may seem very severe, and one has not failed to reproach it to Baucher. But if the horse, by the flexions of neck and jaw, is already displaying a correct "ramener" and is light to the hand, the turning around the haunches, for instance, becomes easy: a simple contact of the acting rein (the left rein if one turns to the right) will suffice most of the time.

The turning around the shoulders is more difficult, and one should not, in the beginning, be too demanding, particularly about the fixity of the "pivot" (the left foreleg in a turning to the right). Although here again, since "ramener" and lightness in hand have brought balance—and Baucher states that they have—the horse should easily master the lateral translation of weight necessary to this rotation.

The rotation of a horse around his shoulders is commonly condemned by the German School because, its Masters say, the pushing effort of the hindquarters, even in a lateral movement, should not be exerted in so slanted a direction as to "ignore" the front legs. But as it happens, it is precisely in the extent to which the inside hind leg (left rear in a turning to right in an "indirect," that is to say left, bending) engages sideways but also *deep forward* that this snag will be avoided. If well performed, the turning around the shoulders is, on the contrary, *highly collective*, as is obvious through the elevation of the withers it provokes.

And, of course, the collecting influence of the movement increases as the bending becomes "regular," that is, direct.

The turning around the shoulders was practiced long before Baucher. By the 16th century, horses were already trained around one pillar, facing it.

The origin of the distrust for this movement probably lies in the rejection, by La Guériniére, of a movement of two tracks, on a circle, the horse's head inside, as practiced by Newcastle. La Guériniére makes us observe, with much sense, that such a movement is constraining and "blocking" for the shoulders (**Ecole de Cavalerie**, Chapter XI, Shoulder-In, Introduction).

But, precisely, the gymnastic of the shoulders is not desired by Baucher in this exercise. It's quite the contrary; speaking of the pirouettes, he states, "The main point is that the part which must be momentarily immobilized remains so" (**Complete Works**, edition 1864, p. 205, translation is mine).

Yet in my opinion, it is somewhat in vain that Baucher tries to work the horse "part by part," for a horse is a whole. The pirouettes show it. While the turning around the shoulders, which is supposed to benefit the haunches only, also works the forehand by the elevation of the withers it provokes, the turning around the haunches, supposed to benefit only the shoulders, also works the hindquarters, since it sits a horse on his rear end.

Baucher wants the pirouettes to be performed *step by step* (that is, one step at a time). In his second "manner," he is still more demanding, since he asks the rider to *check the lightness* after each step, that is, basically, relax the jaw.

Raabe, although extremely meticulous, and probably more so than his teacher Baucher, thinks that a young horse cannot master his balance to such an extent and that one should allow the horse, in the beginning, to more or less "fall" in his pirouettes, making three or four steps. Then, little by little, the horse will be taught how to perform the movement one step at a time.

The Rein Back

The rein back is an exercise upon which Baucher bestowed much importance. Instead of contenting himself with a few steps, as we do nowadays, he would, on the contrary, back up on long distances, and more so, of course, in his first "manner."

To start a rein back, Baucher used his legs first, in order to mobilize the horse, to bring him to "pick up his feet." Whereupon his hand seized the movement so created and gave it a retrograde direction.

This way was not really new. La Guériniére, for instance, would, on foot, give gentle taps with a crop on the front legs of a horse, and when the horse would begin mobilizing himself, he would ask the rider to pull softly on the bridle. The only difference is that Baucher mobilized the horse with his legs where La Guériniére would use a crop.

Let us remark that when the horse is accustomed to the action of backing, La Guériniére would ask it *by the hand only*.

The method advocated by Baucher is, perhaps, logical; it is also very "ticklish" to implement. Indeed, when a horse is solicited by the legs *without any barrier from the hand*, he will first extend a front leg, and it is very difficult to master, with the hand, the movement of this front leg before it touches the ground in order to reverse its direction. I have tried it myself many times and have never succeeded! And one can assess, through this detail, the extraordinary tact of Baucher.

It is, I think, easier to use the hand first in soft enough a way as to not "pull out" the movement by force but strong enough to give the horse notice of the rider's intention *and then only* to come with the legs.

Surprisingly, the way I indicate is more Baucherist than the way that was advocated by Baucher himself, since it abides by the great Baucherist principle: "position precedes action."

Chapter 4

The "Effet d'Ensemble"

The "effet d'ensemble" could as well—and perhaps better—have been called "flexion d'ensemble" (comprehensive flexion), since it comes about only when the partial flexions have been worked out successfully. And it subsequently seems logical to check how they all work when put together.

But the goal of Baucher is more ambitious. He wants, by the "effet d'ensemble, " to create the ideal horse, which will then be ready for everything, a horse which has been trained to bring the "center of forces" to the very same place as the center of gravity, so that the smallest amount of force necessary to create the smallest transfer of weight in a given direction will suffice to create a given movement, and maintain it in perfect regularity to boot.

What "forces" is this about? The forces of propulsion and their counterparts, the forces of restraint or retropropulsion. Any movement implies both of them, even in a forward motion. For instance, when a horse, in an extended trot, stretches a foreleg *and stiffens it* in order to better absorb the kinetic energy of the movement, he puts to work muscles which, from a halt, would have determined a backing.

So Baucher thought that by creating, at a halt, the forces of propulsion with the legs and their counterpart with the hand, one will teach the horse how to bring the center of forces to coincide exactly with the center of gravity and so get the forces to annul each other, which is the condition for immobility to be maintained.

A comparison drawn from modern sport will make the thing still clearer. Let us consider a gymnast as he or she dismounts from the bars and lands. It may happen that the landing is about to be missed, and that the gymnast will have to secure it by an additional step, which would entail a penalty. So although the athlete is *in fact* immobile, it is visible that he or she is fighting to absorb the forces of the momentum, which tend to offset him or her. To be victorious in this fight, the retropropulsive forces will have to be applied at the center of gravity and balance out the momentum in intensity and direction.

And then, having "killed" the momentum, the athlete will release his or her effort in order to bring his or her body into a state of real rest.

This makes clear that the immobility of an "effet d'ensemble" is not a "dead" immobility but a very dynamic one. It will, most of the time, entail a modification in the position of the horse: his back will rise, but rather uniformly, bringing about this "rassembler" (collection) of the first "manner," which so disoriented the practitioners of the Ancient Horsemanship. They compared a "Baucherized" horse to a cat who arches his back, to which the Baucherists would answer that a horse schooled according to the ancient system looked like a cat "about to jump onto the table."

To understand the problem, one has to face a shocking reality: if one wants the rider's legs to be impulsive, they have to foster the *disengagement* of the rear legs rather than their engagement. Engagement, in effect, is never motor, because when a horse engages one hind leg, his foot does not touch the ground. The engagement of one hind leg is always due, at a walk or trot at least, to the disengagement of the other, which *pushes* and is motor.

As long as the hoof of this backward moving leg remains under the horse's body, the "pushing" action is, as a matter of fact, a "pulling" action; it becomes a really "pushing" action when the foot goes behind the vertical of the coxo-femural joint (roughly the edge of the buttock).

So when a horse, at a halt, is submitted to an "effet d'ensemble," he will, at first, tend to open his frame due to the action of the legs, but since the hand forbids this opening, as well as any movement, there will be a fight. The horse will tighten all the muscles of his back, and probably also hold his breath, his front and hind legs acting as opposite "buttresses."

Then he will yield (often with a "sigh"), that is, give up "buttressing," and in so doing tend to *close up front and rear*. The hind legs will move forward, under the body, and, if ever the head was somewhat low (first "manner"), the shoulders will come in an over-hanging position with respect to the front feet. The horse will have taken the position of the "chamois sur un pic" (roebuck on a peak in the Alps).

As we see, an important result of the "effet d'ensemble" is to teach the horse a very sophisticated answer to the legs. When their action is associated to a resistance of the hand, they bring the horse's hind legs under his body, which is primarily anti-impulsive and may be used for "parades." When the barrier of the hand opens, they are supposed to keep their role of forwarding agent.

One assumes that some horses will remain more or less confused and that the respect for the rider's legs, instead of pushing them frankly forward, will, on the contrary, limit the "expression" of the gait, although the rider's hand is fully "giving." Besides, the horse has been accustomed by the flexions to keep his "ramener" even if the hand has given, and this will be one more possible reason for him to display some lack of generosity in his movement. Of course, if the training reaches its goal, it will, on the contrary, result in a perfectly light, perfectly balanced horse whose movements have *the regularity of a clock*.

Now, what if the horse, in his desire for forward movement, opens his frame? The rider's legs will have to prevent it. The temptation will then be great to use them *permanently*, and the rider will, after the word of General L'Hotte already quoted, "have nothing in the hand, but carry the horse with his legs."

And this is all the more likely to happen as a second and dreadful embarrassment is going to come up: repeated opposition of hand and legs will, in effect, completely "erase" the impulsive meaning of the latter.

Indeed, let's face another piece of shocking evidence; if the rider's hand (although very awkward a brake) may claim some physical, physiological power in restraining a horse, the rider's legs have none as concerns their impulsive mission; they draw all their possible power from conditioning. Horses are not born with a little accelerator in the ribs. We have to create this accelerator, and this process is 100% *psychological*. It pertains to the field of conditioning reflexes, which was first explored by Pavlov.

In his celebrated experiments, Pavlov would make a dog salivate (natural reflex) by presenting him with a piece of meat (natural signal) as he rang a bell. He did this 80 times in a row. By the 81st experiment, he omitted the piece of meat and only rang the bell, *and the dog would salivate all the same*. This salivation was not natural;

[48]

it was conditioned.

In the same way, the association to the rider's legs of a whip or spurs will rapidly realize the conditioning to the leg of the locomotive reflex of the horse. The legs will take on the *same meaning* as the spurs or whip, and, if the conditioning is correct, will provoke the same *reflexive response*. The legs are the bell of Pavlov's experiments.

The conditioning, once realized, is rather fragile. It will have to be carefully protected and even sometimes "refreshed," since two dangers threaten it: oblivion on one hand and accidental "erasure" by another conditioning on the other. This is precisely what happens if one *systematically* associates the hand, *a natural signal of inhibition of the motive reflexes*, to the legs, a neutral signal available for any type of conditioning. The legs will take on the *same meaning as the hand*, that is, an inhibitive meaning.

At the time of Baucher, Pavlov was unknown. But nowadays, all this should be common wisdom. *Alas!*

But let's come back to the "effet d'ensemble." The principle of opposing retropropulsive and propulsive forces was—perhaps— valid; it was the means which were questionable. In this respect, the use of the pillars (which Baucher despised) by the ancient school was much more logical than the "effet d'ensemble," since it opposed two natural means of restraint and propulsion: the pillars and the whip, which didn't have to be conditioned to become effective. In a "succinct exposition of the method by questions and answers," Baucher asks, "Is it not to be feared that the horse may become insensitive to the legs and lose all activity for accelerated movements?" The answer is, "Since all these means serve only to keep the horse in the most perfect equilibrium, promptness of movements ought necessarily to be the result of it, and, consequently, the horse *will be disposed to respond to the progressive contact of the legs, when the hand does not oppose it"* (italics are mine).

So be it; but what if the horse no longer understands what this progressive contact means? Let me recount a personal experience.

I used to have a school horse who was "lazy" or, rather, who had been made so by dint of poor equitation. So I would demonstrate to my students what the proper conditioning to the legs should be by using the crop two or three times in strict conjunction with the legs, and, subsequently, I would ride the horse carefully avoiding two errors. The first error would have been to use my legs and my hand together; the second would have been to associate, even for a short time, a steady action of legs to a steady speed (the aids are a means for transition, not for maintenance; when they have reached their goal, they must quit; maintenance pertains to the horse).

After a few minutes of this riding, my horse would be sufficiently aroused to allow me what follows. I would come into the middle of the ring, stop, completely drop the reins, wait a few seconds, and then, by the mere pressure of my heels, start a canter from a halt without any intermediary steps of walk or strides of trot. Applause.

Then I would say, "I am going to erase this conditioning before your very eyes." I would go half a perimeter of the arena at a trot, keeping my legs actively on and preventing, with my hands, the horse from accelerating.

Then I would come into the middle of the arena, stop, drop the reins, and try, with my heels, to start a canter again. But this time, I wouldn't get any canter, nor any trot, nor even a walk; *the horse would stay still!*

It has been said that Baucher had powerful legs, but this does not hold water, since shouting won't help if one applies in Greek to somebody who does not speak Greek.

So it seems that the use of the mere leg in the "effet d'ensemble" was rather theoretical and that the spurs would be used systematically. Raabe, an adept of the first "manner," used the spurs (against the hand) at the girth for the yielding of the jaw (hence the "ramener") and back from the girth for the "rassembler" (collection). For him, the "effet d'ensemble" on the leg without use of the spurs was just meant to calm a horse, not to collect him.

Speaking of the spurs, Baucher did make elaborate use of them. He would use them to moderate the ardor of a high-spirited horse, to stop short a canter, to rein back *in a total release of hand*, to give impulsion by the "soft attacks" (second "manner"), and last but not least to "enclose" a horse ("rassembler," that is, collection) by the "brisk attacks" (first "manner"). But, apart from the "brisk attacks" (and still, in a very limited way), he never elaborated on the diverse modalities of this use. I shall try to remedy this lacuna.

The spurs can be used either by "pinching" or by "poking." When they "pinch" (progressive pressure by the neck of the spur, avoiding if possible any "stinging"), their effect is *inhibitive*. When they "poke," their effect is impulsive, energizing, or, better, *rousing*.

"Pinchings" and "pokings" may be soft or strong. A soft pinching can aid the hand in relaxing the jaw; it can also *start* a rein back upon the hand's resisting. It can also move the haunches laterally.

A strong pinching is used in the "effet d'ensemble," more particularly in the second "manner." It calms the horse and in the meantime *prevents him from opening his frame*. As a matter of fact, after an "effet d'ensemble," the rider may drop the reins first; if he keeps the steady pressure of the spurs, the horse will keep his "ramener" and sometimes *spontaneously mobilize his jaw* (although the reins lie on his neck).

Little attacks (the hand giving or resisting depending on the horse's reaction and the rider's intentions) should not throw a horse out of himself but increase its activity.

Brisk attacks were used in the first " manner," *against the hand* and after the "effet d'ensemble" to further "enclose" the horse. As a matter of fact, given the limits of the "effet d'ensemble," they were the main "tool" for collection. Writes Maxime Gaussen in the preface to **Passe-Temps Equestres** (1840), "It is really strange to see the horses trained by Baucher 'sit' upon the vigorous attack of the spurs, provided it was accompanied with the slightest opposition of the hand."

It is important to notice that in the "attacks," the rider's calves are not removed from the horse's sides. Only the rider's heels are involved in the process; Baucher even states that before their being used, the spurs must be brought "one hair" from the sides of the horse. Raabe, a very meticulous and systematic adept of the first "manner," explained the efficacy of the "attacks" by the influence they have on the diaphragm of a horse (**Methode de Haute Ecole de Raabe**, General Decarpentry, p. 143). His explanations are very convincing.

In his second "manner, " Baucher recommended a very careful progression in the use of the spurs. The horse should first stand the graduated pressure of the bare legs of the rider; then one will use spurs whose rowels have been covered by a sheath of leather. Then only will one make use of the bare rowels. This careful progression must have taken place before the "official" start of the second "manner," since Raabe already mentions it.

Chapter 5

The Second "Manner"

"Hand without legs - Legs without hand"

On November 9, 1913, in Kenitra (Morocco), a 16 hand, blood bay "Anglo-Barb" (TB/Barb cross) by the name of *Robersart 2* managed to: compete in a jumping show; circulate almost all day long in a horse fair organized by his trainer and rider, French Captain Marcel Beudant; offer an exhibition of "High School" riding; and then, under a weight of 154 pounds, take part in a 3-mile cross-country race against 11 other horses of the same breed and beat them by 60 lengths (172 meters, or 188 yards).

Wrote a bystander, Captain Dutertre of the 1st Chasseur d'Afrique (1st African Rangers), about *Robersart's* High School exhibition: "Without losing for one instant his lightness, *Robersart*, who looked absolutely free, alternated in a perfect 'continuum,' piaffe, passage, passage on two tracks, pirouettes and reversed pirouettes at a passage, trot and canter backward, flying changes at every stride of canter, Spanish walk and trot, and outrightly extended Spanish trot. The gaits, like the transitions between different airs, would come about without one's noticing any movement of the rider's body, hands or legs, or even any contraction of his face revealing an effort."

By March 14, 1915, *Robersart's* work had improved in sophistication. His feats included: at a passage *whose cadence, elevation, and length of stride would vary at his rider's request,* counter-changes of hand, half-pirouettes, half-reversed pirouettes, half-passes on a circle and at a canter, counter-changes of hand *without changing the lead,* flying changes cantering backwards, transitions from a canter backward to a passage, etc., notwithstanding, of course, all the trot or canter movements with stretching of a foreleg at will.

All the onlookers noticed the suppleness, lightness, precision, impulsion, and *good humor* of *Robersart,* who was ridden *with a simple snaffle,* and the calm, relaxation, and invisibility of the aids of his rider, *who rode without stirrups!*

On September 17, 1917, after a seven month stay in a hospital, including 92 days of complete immobilization in a cast, Beudant, too sore to wear riding boots, rode his horse *Iris* "impromptu," in slippers and without a crop.

Iris, a 15 hand, bay Anglo-Arab, had been out of training for the same length of time; yet, mouthed with a simple snaffle, he performed, without flinching, a program similar to *Robersart*'s with the same invisibility of the rider's aids.

Shortly after this, Beudant was obliged to sell *Iris,* because he had to go to Paris in order to further his medical treatment. *Iris'* new owner would engage the horse in five flat races; *he won all five.*

Before quitting Morocco, Beudant had asked Veterinary Colonel Monod and Captain Desfeux, chief of the Military Remount of Casablanca, to attest that *Iris* would perform canter flying changes at every stride on a circle as well as on a straight line and canter on three legs (on each lead) and pass from a canter forward to a canter backward on three legs, the raised leg remaining perfectly stretched.

Wrote a Lieutenant Garineau on August 1, 1915, "Captain Beudant's system of training, based on collection, consists in destroying all the resistances of a horse by means of the appropriate suppling. When the horse reaches the 'rassembler,' he delivers all his forces, doing nothing by rote. It then suffices to know how to utilize it."

This is sheer Baucherism. But Beudant was a Baucherist of the second "manner."

Notwithstanding his immense talent, Beudant was very deserving in doing so well, for he had been his own teacher. He had learned the "method" *by the book only.*

Which book? That of General Faverot de Kerbrech, **Methodic Training of the Riding Horse, after the last teaching of Baucher gathered by one of his students** (1891, translation of the title is mine).

General de Kerbrech played a key role in the development of Baucher's second "manner." As a captain in the 1860s, he was one of Baucher's preferred students. As a colonel, he would command the 23rd Regiment of Dragoons, where 20-year-old Beudant engaged in 1883. In 1885, when Kerbrech departed from the Regiment, Beudant was a simple NCO. He never got the occasion to be introduced to his colonel, let alone take lessons from him.

But let us come back to the development of Baucherism and take the events in chronological order. The 12th edition of the "Method" came out in 1864. Its first readers were probably puzzled, as they discovered that after the conclusion (chapter XXXII), the book goes on, and that it is not about simple "appendices" of more or less anecdotal value. Far from it: the matter is brand new and, at times, seems to contradict the rest of the book.

The summary of this addendum, a book within the book, reads:
• perfect equilibrium of the first genre: hand without legs, legs without hand,

• three new effects of hand: 1) to obtain a right division of the weight, 2) to restore the harmony of forces, 3) to give the positions useful for changes of direction by the outside rein, 4) departures into canter and flying changes (hand without legs, legs without hand),

• on the separation of force from movement,

• progression of the training (translation of these subtitles is mine).

Coming back to the first 32 chapters, the reader would then understand better why the material, although familiar, seemed at times slightly "offset" with respect to the previous, rather dogmatic "method." Why, for instance, the chapter on the "effet d'ensemble" now seemed full of reserves (nay, innuendos) about its possible dangers ("let us not, therefore, multiply beyond measure the 'effets d'ensemble' lest we bring uncertainty into the movements of the horse," p. 97). Why, also, the flexion of the jaw took precedence over the flexion of the neck, and why the new wording of "mobility of the jaw" was used to describe it. The second "manner" was born.

It proceeded from the discovery, by Baucher, of a state of balance he called "equilibrium of the first genre." This supreme equilibrium is not *an* equilibrium; it is *the* equilibrium, the same no matter what, regardless of the gait, movement, and even speed as long as one remains in the realm of collected horsemanship, that is, High School.

Writes he, "The ancient horsemanship would work the movement by the movement, by giving the instinctive forces of a horse a more or less correct direction; but it was never capable of making light an ill-built horse, because it did not know the means for changing its natural balance.

"I had understood that the education of a horse lies in his

equilibrium, and all my studies aimed at finding the way to improve the defective balance of a horse, since I was convinced that a well-balanced horse was almost trained ['dressé'], and yet I had only succeeded in obtaining the equilibrium of the second genre.

"...With this equilibrium...I could get, at times, much lightness, but this lightness would then subside due to a new movement, a change of direction.

"True, I would promptly destroy this momentary resistance, and I would thus acquire a great lightness by correcting the horse's position; though even, there had been a breach of lightness, which could at times make the movement look less graceful, the work less accurate; furthermore, in spite of the well known progresses of my horses, I would know every day a new 'desideratum,' whereas today, once their education is complete, I have nothing more to desire from them.

"What I obtain from the horses I am riding now, by giving them this perfect equilibrium, allows me to say that if I could anew show the public my former horses, everybody would acknowledge the truth of what I am bringing forth" (op. cit., pp. 171-173, this and all future translations are mine).

This equilibrium of the first genre is obtained when a horse is working in a state of permanent lightness regardless of the evolutions he is called on to perform, that is, if at any time, the rider can check, through a "half-tension" of the reins, that the jaw can be mobilized. By "half-tension," which is the term used by Baucher, one should understand "soft tension."

What if the jaw resists? All depends on the kind of resistance.

"The effect of the hand will be different depending on whether it has to fight the resistance of the weight or of the force. To recognize the cause of this resistance, the rider will slowly and gradually bring his hand nearer his body. If the resistance is inert, it proceeds from the wrongly distributed weight; in this case, the hand will act through a half-halt, prompt and proportioned to the intensity of the resistance. If this half-halt does not suffice, it will be followed with a second, a third, up to the disappearance of this inert resistance. These half-halts, practiced with a force directed upwards, destroy the resistances of the weight without overly 'sitting' ['acculer'] the horse; if the resistance proceeds from the force, the hand will act by reiterated *vibrations*, until lightness is restored..." (12th edition, p. 177).

The Baucherist "half-halt" is not exactly that described by La Guérinière in **Ecole de Cavalerie** (1731).

"The vocable 'half-halt'...gives only an imperfect idea of what it must represent. This term implies a slowing down. I kept it to not change an expression consecrated by the usage. I make use of it only to describe a transference of weight, on the express condition that one does not diminish the action proper to the movement. If the half-halt is done at a halt, it should in no case bring about a backing" (op. cit., footnote, p. 177).

To practice a half-halt at a halt is indeed quite paradoxical, but the paradox lies only in the words. The Baucherist half-halt is nothing else than the action by which a rider upholds the forehand of his mount. Its purpose is not so much to raise the horse's head as to elevate his *withers*. This elevation of the withers creates the transference of weight looked for without influencing the speed, that is, the action.

Still, the half-halt of La Guérinière is not that different from Baucher's, since La Guérinière states that one can repeat it often *without breaking the gait* (**Ecole de Cavalerie**, p. 190). Simply, La

[58]

Guérinière does not go to the extreme of the concept as Baucher does.

The reader will have noticed that in order to check the possible resistances, the rider is requested to bring his hand "nearer his body." This comes apparently as a denial of Baucher's "last words" (which I evoked in the first chapter) as reported by General L'Hotte: "'Always this'—and he immobilized my hand under the pressure of his— 'never that'—and he drew my hand nearer my chest". But it is not so. As a matter of fact, the (soft) backward movement of the rider's hand advocated by Baucher is meant to establish the so-called "half-tension," upon which any well-trained horse should mobilize his lower jaw. If this mobilization does not come about, the hand acts by vibrations and for this *fixes itself.*

Writes General de Kerbrech, "If the hand does not meet with lightness upon the half-tension of the reins, it maintains this half-tension *with a slightly increased intensity.*

"This 'slow force' suffices generally to get the yielding, especially when there is only a little laziness and inattention with the horse.

"But it may happen that in spite of a fairly long waiting and the persistence of the rider's solicitation, the relaxation of the jaw does not come about.

"This would mean that there are resistances serious enough to require more efficient procedures.

"...One fights the resistances of weight by the half-halt, the resistances of force by the vibrations" (op. cit., pp. 10-11).

Of course, as the dressage training of the horse progresses, vibrations and half-halts will progressively lose their importance to the profit of the mere *contraction of the hand, in place.*

Writes General de Kerbrech, "When the training of the horse is completed, there remains only to make him become very keen to the aids, so as not to be any longer obliged to move in a noticeable way the hand or the legs in order to communicate to him our orders.

"The hand then must abstain from any action which would look like a punishment, like the half-halt or even the vibration.

"It must then only act through mellow and immobile indications" (op. cit., p. 188).

Yet it is Captain Beudant who gave the best definition of what this action of hand should be. After having quoted the last words of Baucher as reported by General L'Hotte, he added, "Here lies the secret which alone allows one to master a horse's mouth, whether outside or in High School riding; that is to say, to obtain the relative lightness which suffices to check a bolter, or the almost complete lightness which, in High School work, places a horse at the disposal of his rider (*the hand acts without taking from the impulsion*). *But one has to know how to fix the hand.*

"Fixing the hand is not giving the horse a support with the bit in order to help him gallop, because this would mean pulling, opposing to the horse's mouth a force equal to that he himself is using. One succeeds, on the contrary, by fixing the hand absolutely without any pulling and by squeezing the reins with one's fingers *in a convulsive way if necessary*, so as to prevent the hand from being attracted by any force: the horse's mouth, or the rider's wrist. ..With the fixed hand, it is the horse who *yields to himself*, who rewards himself, who takes pleasure in chewing his bit, therefore giving suppleness and mellowness to his mouth" (**Dressage du Cheval de Selle**, 1929, p. 60).

This fixity of the hand requires an education. It is not a "passive" fixity, only meant to give the horse a support with the bit, as in the

German horsemanship; it is a very "active" fixity which allows the hand, upon the mouth's yielding, to avoid any recoil movement, since the rider's arm was not involved in the action, only his fingers, thus enabling the horse to enjoy an *automatic reward*.

This fixity is expressed by the requirement not to "pull." Not to pull does not mean that one does not apply, at times, a traction on the reins. Far from it; it means that one does it in such a manner as being at any time capable of *checking this traction, annulling it instantly*.

The only way to reach this goal is, after having confirmed the contact with the mouth by a soft backing movement of the hand, to squeeze one's fingers on the rein as if the target of their action was not the mouth but the rein itself. One knows that one was "pulling" if, upon the mouth's yielding, one's hand moves back, *ever so slightly*.

This fixity of the hand is difficult to acquire and *has always been the "ticklish" point of the Baucherist technique*.

One has to acquire the "knack," lest one produce the "clattering" mouth which has always been the plague of Baucherist apprentices.

Let's come now to the centerpiece of this second "manner," the principle of "hand without legs, legs without hand."

One will first notice, for the record, that "legs" is plural, whereas "hand" is always singular. This is because the rider at the time of Baucher used only one hand—the left— to steer his horse. Both reins of curb were held by the left hand. As for the reins of snaffle, they were let loose or held by the right hand.

Baucher was led to set forth this principle out of a concern for "economy of the means." Indeed, if one cares about lightness, one will try to avoid "bombarding" the horse with forceful and sometimes *contradictory* signals. If one succeeds in keeping a horse in proper balance through a combination of aids (the aids acting simultaneously), it means that perhaps the legs have had to correct the errors or excesses of the hand, and vice versa. These errors have been unaccounted for; the result is safe, but the manner was coarse. There has been lack of opportunity. If the hand or the legs act alone, they will have to reach their *optimal threshold of efficacy*. The rider will become efficient *and subtle*; the horse will become attentive *and calm*.

But the horse will become not only calm but also *highly sensitive to the legs*, since hand and legs will no longer *erase each other's conditioning*, an occurrence in which, as we have seen when treating the "effet d'ensemble," the legs are more at a disadvantage than the hand.

And so a new style of riding will become possible: riding in the release of hand *and legs*, that is, in the "release of aids," the horse being left in "liberty on parole" and the aids wielded *only for transitions*: the legs (alone) for the "up" transitions, and the hand (alone) for the "down" transitions. When there is no need for a modification of the speed, movement, gait, or direction of the horse, the aids *remain silent*.

Writes Baucher, "By using only one force at a time, whether that of the legs to give impulsion or that of the hand to operate the transference of weight needed by such and such a movement, such and such a gait, the rider can assess instantly the degree of appropriateness he has displayed.

"If he commits an error, he can correct it at once; he knows its cause, and the poor horse, being no longer tossed about between these two opposite wills of hand and legs, identifies himself so much with the thoughts of his master that soon these two intelligences make only one, *the horse keeping his perfect equilibrium without the help of his rider's hand or legs* (op. cit., 12th edition, p. 175, italics are mine).

The expression "release of the aids," which I have used in the lines above, is the translation I think the more appropriate of "descente des aides." "Descente" in French means descent, going down, downward slope, etc. But it also means subsidence, and it is in this way that it should be understood in the expression "descente des aides," that is, subsidence, abatement of the aids.

As a matter of fact, these two possible meanings, that of lowering and that of subsiding, apply equally for the celebrated "descente de main" (release of the hand) of La Guérinière, because in the ancient horsemanship, the hand was always held high, so its lowering and the release of its action were synonymous.

This is why "descente de main" was expressed by "lowering of the hand" in the translation of the ninth edition of Baucher which appears in Hilda Nelson's book **Baucher, The Man and His Method** which I mentioned in my first chapter. And since there is no "descente de jambes" (release of the legs) in Baucher's first "manner," this translation is acceptable, although it does not give any account of the notion of "subsidence" which is inherent in the "lowering" of the hand.

But when it comes to the legs, their "descente" is absolutely not a stretching down; it is a release in their action.

Now, how does all this, "hand without legs, etc." and the "release of the aids," conciliate with the "effet d'ensemble?" Surprisingly well, and this is why.

[63]

The "effet d'ensemble" in the second "manner" lost much of its importance. In the first "manner," Baucher states that the 'effet d'ensemble' "ought to precede and follow each exercise within the graduated limit assigned to it" (op. cit., 6th edition, 1844, p. 160). In the 12th edition, whose first part is but a "corrected text" and not a new cast, the "effet d'ensemble" has its role reduced to the "preparation" of each exercise, and the chapter devoted to it ends with this bizarre warning: "Let us therefore not multiply beyond measure the 'effet d'ensemble,' lest we bring uncertainty into the horse's movements; and moreover, let us hold as a principle that all the expenses of force, all the useless translations of weight, are harmful to the education of the animal, as well as to its structure."

In the second part of the 12th edition, consecrated to the "new means," one finds this: "to stop his horse, the rider will at first use the 'effet d'ensemble' (graduated opposition of hand and legs); but soon, the hand will suffice to stop a horse straight in his shoulders and haunches" (op. cit., p. 209).

In fact, what one sees emerging as one reads the texts is that the "effet d'ensemble" still applies when the matter is stability, that is, at a halt *to calm a horse* or in motion *to restore the regularity of a gait*, whereas the principle "hand without legs, legs without hand" applies always to *any transition* from one speed, one gait, one movement to another speed, gait, or movement.

States Baucher, "Since the combined action of the legs and the hand *immobilizes* a horse, one understands by the same token that, when it is about *movement*, one should not use the same means" (**Complete Works**, 1864, p. 209).

Let us also notice, as concerns the possible danger of "erasure" of the impulsive conditioning of the legs which is inherent to the "effet d'ensemble," that in the second "manner," the "effet d'ensemble" mandatorily implies the spur. General Faverot de Kerbrech always uses the term "effet d'ensemble sur l'eperon," that is, "effet d'ensemble *on the spur.*" Now the spur, as long as it does not "pinch" too strongly, has an unquestionable *forwarding* effect, and its opposition to the hand realizes exactly (and better) what Baucher had in mind by the start of his method.

Surprisingly, when it comes to a "strong pinching," the "effet d'ensemble" does not even deny the principle "hand without legs, etc.," for this principle tends to avoid any *opposition* between hand and legs, and in the case of a strong pinching with the spurs, their action, being *inhibitive,* just reinforces that of the hand.

In the second "manner," the "rassembler" (collection) is no longer the result of a plain opposition of hand and legs ("effet d'ensemble"), but the result of *alternate* actions of legs and hand (hand without legs, etc.). Writes Gen. de Kerbrech, " . . . the effet d'ensemble quiets, extinguishes or regularizes; the 'rassembler' animates, arouses, stirs up the activity, gives life and brilliancy" (op. cit., p. 31).

Let us observe here, to be completely clear about the remaining role of the "effet d'ensemble" in the second "manner," that its use applies to a horse *who has still not reached the equilibrium of the "first genre"* (overcoming and calming of a turbulent horse), or who, for some reason, has temporarily lost it (regularizing of the gaits).

The "effet d'ensemble" is therefore: 1) occasional, 2) momentary, and 3) always followed with a *total release of the aids.*

About the principle "hand without legs, legs without hand," which is the blunt opposite of the "effet d'ensemble" and takes, by far, precedence over it, it must be stressed that the Baucherists of the second "manner" were all *very serious about it* and observed it *religiously*. Writes Gen. de Kerbrech, "One must apply from the beginning the principle 'hand without legs, legs without hand' as often and as long as one does not need to resort to the 'effet d'ensemble on the spur,' in order to prevent a fight or to make the animal feel the power of the man" (op. cit., p. 89).

This principle is tirelessly stressed with a flawless coherence on occasion of the multiple occurrences of the training of a horse throughout the 198 pages of Gen. de Kerbrech's book. I cannot quote all of these, but I entertained myself making a list of the pages on which they appear, one or several times: 93, 96, 97, 107, 109, 110, 112, 116, 118, 130, 132, 133, 136, 138, 139, 140, 141, 142, 152, 154, 155, 156, 159, 161, 170, 171, and 186.

This is so much so that by the end of the book, Gen. de Kerbrech feels a need to soften somewhat a position which could be considered too dogmatic: "The principle 'hand without legs, legs without hand' must be applied as often as possible, more particularly in the beginning, but it is not an absolute. One therefore ought not to make out of it a system without which there would be only failure. *One must limit oneself to put it into practice as long as there is no serious reason to depart from it*; but there comes a time in the training and later in the wielding of a trained horse when there is some reason to the contrary to combine effects of the lower and upper aids.

"For instance, when a horse already very advanced in his preparation does not become light upon a delicate solicitation of the hand, it is proper to apply a slight pressure with the legs and to come at once with a soft attack with the spurs, if the jaw does not mobilize itself immediately..." (op. cit., p. 91).

Now I ask the reader to consider carefully the part of the quote

I have stressed: "one must limit oneself to put it into practice. . . " It is the translation, word by word, of the French "on doit se borner à le mettre en pratique tant qu'il n'y a pas de raisons sérieuses de s'en écarter."

Hilda Nelson, in her significant (and welcome) book **Baucher, The Man and His Method**, came up with the following translation: "One must refrain from putting it into practice as long as there is no real reason to use it." *It is an unfortunate mistranslation which makes Faverot de Kerbrech say the opposite of what he really meant.*

This is very regrettable, because this amounts to limiting Baucher's message to his first "manner," since the essential mutation which led to the second "manner," the principle of "hand without legs, legs without hand" and the subsequent loss of prominence of the "effet d'ensemble," is then dramatically denied its importance.

Baucher's work (in my opinion) has to be understood as a "continuum" which takes its true and definitive meaning by the very end of its process.

To this mistranslation, which is a real "slip of the pen" from a scholar perfectly versed in the French language, I would be tempted to give a "Freudian" explanation. It reveals, in my opinion, the deep rooting in the subconscious of most riders, especially in the United States, of the belief that collection *cannot* be obtained save by a plain opposition of propulsive and retropropulsive aids. For those riders, riding in lightness (i.e., with as little constraint as possible) shocks, if only secretly.

Baucher himself was probably the first to be embarrassed by his new discovery and the character it bore of forswearing of his very doctrine. Writes he: "This new axiom was so much in formal opposition to what I had myself professed and practiced all my life that, in spite of the marvelous results I was obtaining from it, I wanted to have glaring proof of its truth.

"So before delivering this edition to the public, I gathered five deft riders whose loyalty and discretion I knew I could trust, and I made them experiment with it.

"Success fulfilled my expectations. I could convince myself that the long practice I have in the wielding of my aids did not make me believe this last discovery more fruitful than it really was. Each of these gentlemen handed me a written report on the application they were making of it under my eyes, and I asked M. Faverot de Kerbrech for permission to publish his work, which may serve as a complement and a development for my new means" (op. cit., 12th edition, pp. 185-186).

Baucher felt so much the necessity of being backed up in this enterprise that he published not only the text of Faverot de Kerbrech but also the works of two other students of his, MM. d'Estiennes and de Sainte Reine.

This feeling was not misleading, since the principle immediately triggered hostility and distrust. "Then Baucher is no longer Baucher," exclaimed Gerhardt, a faithful of the first "manner." Fillis (pupil of a pupil of Baucher) states, "It is simply absurd to say that the 'complete rassembler' can be obtained by the hands without the legs, or by the legs without the hands" (**Riding and Breaking**, p. 340).

General L'Hotte himself tried to minimize the importance of the discovery: "To the enclosure of the horse, maintained in the embrace of the aids, succeeded the use of the hand without the legs, the legs without the hand, suitable in fact more to ordinary rather than academic riding. Subsequently, this way of using the aids was no longer recommended but for riders of little skill, to simplify their actions and avoid the faults resulting from their lack of accord" (**Un Officier de Cavalerie**, p. 135).

Beudant, with much humor and a delightful hypocrisy, does not hesitate to place himself in this latter category. Writes he (in **Main Sans Jambes**, p. 15), "All in all, especially for non-expert riders, the wiser way is to limit oneself, like me, to using the hand without the legs, and the legs without the hand."

Chapter 6

The Second "Manner"

The lifting of the neck

W̶e now come to the most controversial feature of the second "manner," the lifting of the neck.

Although it is, with the new principle "hand without legs, legs without hand," the most obvious modification of the "method," Baucher does not elaborate much on it in the 12th edition. Nowhere, for instance, can one find the heading "lifting of the neck" above a simple paragraph, let alone a chapter. To my knowledge, apart from a drawing featuring a rider practicing, on foot, a forceful elevation of a horse's neck (this is about the study of backing up) and two lines on page 208, the only elaborate description of this proceeding is one paragraph in the chapter dedicated to the "separation of force from movement," which reads: "Although certain persons little versed in my principles blame the position in which I set the neck and head of a horse, I hold that it is indispensable to give them all the elevation they can take by acting upwards with the wrists. *One should not be afraid of the horizontal position that the head takes obligatorily...* Then it is, that one must *relax the jaw*, whose mellow mobility allows the horse to set his head by himself in the academic position. This apparently indirect means is the only one to give grace and a constant lightness in all the horse's movements" (12th edition, p. 184, translations and italics are mine).

So once again, we have to resort to Gen. Faverot de Kerbrech, who, fortunately, is more explicit on this subject. Let us take a few excerpts from his book **Methodic Training of the Riding-Horse, after the last teachings of Baucher gathered by one of his students:**"In the beginning, one endeavors to make turnings with a high and more or less horizontal head. But as the schooling of the horse progresses, one must execute them with the 'ramener' [the academic vertical position of the head]" (p. 102).

"The important point—at a halt particularly, but in motion as well—is to obtain first the lightness as the horse has his head high. The 'ramener' comes later by virtue of the mellowness of the mouth. But it is necessary that the jaw yield first, the neck being very high, and without the head making any movement" (p. 110).

"This recommendation of asking first for lightness, the neck being very much withheld, applies to the curb as well as the snaffle. One relaxes the jaw, the head being high and almost horizontal. Then only should one allow it to near the perpendicular line. But with a horse prepared in this way, the 'ramener' comes about fast and soon becomes easy to maintain" (p. 111).

"**How should one raise the neck** - During all this first period of the training, one must seek to raise the neck as much as possible. It is upon the weight that one acts by demanding this elevation; but it is necessary that while one is transferring it backwards, *the force that provides the movement be in no way diminished*; by contrast, while giving the action, producing the force which pushes, it is necessary that this very force *attract in the direction of the movement only the small quantity of weight needed by the movement*, and that the translations of weight remain equally easy in every direction, *after as well as before the movement was obtained.*

"When a horse shows a strong tendency to collapse in his neck, one must hold one's wrists very high, above the ears if necessary, until the jaw has softly yielded in this position. One then yields, but one takes again as soon as the head drops down, keeping the hand constantly elevated to prevent the horse from 'burying' himself.

"With such a horse, one must keep working at a halt and at short gaits for a very long time and take the curb again only after one has obtained a constant and very easy elevation on the snaffle" (pp. 116-117).I would also like to quote here—and so put an end to this list of references—Captain Marcel Beudant, who so brilliantly illustrated this style of horsemanship: "In High Equitation, in order for balance to come about, the head must be vertical or thereabout, as it remains very elevated.

"This position comes naturally as a result of the mellowness of the mouth, and in the beginning, one must be very watchful not to try to give it before having obtained the mobility of the jaw, the head remaining high and even horizontal. Never try to place the head before having obtained lightness.

"With a long neck the vertical position comes easily, but with a short neck, and if one wants the head to remain high, this latter will come to a lesser degree and with more difficulty nearer the vertical. Now one should not let the horse 'bury himself' and lower the neck in order to set the head vertically, because the lower the neck, the farther away the head is from the body, the less it is possible to achieve balance and to 'sit' the horse in order to make him execute brilliant movements" (**Main sans Jambes**, p. 36).

The very notion of the lifting of the neck is nowadays rather shocking for the lay riding public. This proceeds partly from the erroneous opinion that when a horse raises his neck, he hollows his back, thus making collection impossible. This conception is seriously upheld in many a good riding treatise and found an unexpected defender in the person of General Decarpentry (**Academic Equitation**, chapter V).

Before going any further, let us acknowledge that General Decarpentry—whose social rank protected him from this kind of 'promiscuity'—probably never had to haggle with a horse dealer. It is indeed well known that any horse dealer who wants to make a 16 hand horse look like he is 16.2 will raise the horse's head to a suitable maximum, *because raising the neck raises the withers.*

And if the withers rise, then the back can definitely not flatten.

Besides, one can convince oneself of the verity of what I am saying. Place a horse (I mean a *sound* horse; I will explain why later) on a cement slab and measure his size in three different positions: 1) as he is eating some hay on the ground, 2) with a normal position of head, and 3) with a very high head. You will get three different sizes, such as 15.3, 16.1, and 16.2 hands, the last corresponding to the high position of the head (Fig. 14).

I specified that the horse has to be sound because if you do not see the withers rise as the neck is pushed up, it probably means that they are *locked* (and by the way, this could explain the riding problems you have with your mount). Any good chiropractor can take care of the problem.[1]

Another experiment: on the same cement slab, measure your horse unmounted, and then mounted. You will get two different measures, *the smaller being that of the mounted horse.*

Why is that so? Because a horse has no clavicle (collar bone). And whereas *there is a* bone-to-bone connection between the top of the croup and the ground, there is no *bone-to-bone connection from*

Fig. 14

the withers down. The withers and the front of the rib cage are literally floating between the shoulder blades, to which they are fixed only by muscles and ligaments. This liaison is supple (which is an advantage for the horse at liberty), but it is also weak (which is a disadvantage for the mounted horse, who has to bear the rider's weight).

Given this phenomenon, one understands that any lifting of the withers is highly profitable for the mounted horse, if only because it helps him fight the crushing effect of the rider's weight, and in so doing retrieve *under the saddle the equilibrium he had in liberty.*

Now let us consider the notion of "collection." Collection, in essence, lies in the permanent engagement of the hindquarters, that is, the tipping under of the pelvis. This tipping under brings about an arching of the lumbar vertebrae, which *tends to help the horse in raising his withers*. So much so that engagement of the hindquarters and lifting of the withers are almost synonymous, and the feeling of "lowering" of the haunches, subsequent to any good collection, proceeds as much, if not more, from the raising of the front end than from the bending of the hocks.

But I will not discuss here the bending of the hocks, since it is not relevant to our subject. All the same, I will not explain why General Decarpentry came to a different — and to my view, erroneous — conclusion, since it would carry us too far away, to little avail; I just hope I have convinced my readers. Let me only say this: if people are so easily convinced that the lifting of the neck entails a hollowing of the back, it is because this is the case with the human body, and as it happens, it is precisely because humans have clavicles.

I have spoken of the lifting of the neck of an unmounted horse. Now what if the rider tries to do it from horseback? The result, at first glance, might seem more questionable.

Upon having his head lifted, a horse can react in at least two ways. He can yield only with his neck, by "hollowing" it, giving it a "ewe like" shape; in this case, he will not lift his withers. He also can resist with his neck, "solidify" it, thus raising his withers. He can also do a little of both, which is most likely to happen.

But in any event, he will take the easiest solution. If he is unmounted, the demand of elevation being made from the ground, experience shows that the easy solution is *always* the elevation of the withers.

But when the attempt at elevating the neck is made from horseback the situation is very different, if only because the rider no longer benefits from the "fulcrum" of the ground. As a matter of fact, he is now using the back of the horse as a fulcrum, and this, at first glance, seems more likely to hollow the back than to round it.

However, experience shows that, at a halt at least, the lifting of the head from horseback entails some lifting of the withers; this is why: As they are pushed down by the rider's weight, the vertebrae of the withers "close in," which means that their vertical processes come closer to each other. If, then, the cervical vertebrae, those of the neck, increase their natural "ewe like" shape because the rider is lifting the head, these processes of the withers will "close in" still more, and they will tend to "kiss," which always provokes a very sharp pain.

The horse will, of course, try to avoid, if he can, being placed in this situation and will therefore respond to the elevation of the head in the same way as if unmounted. One should also bear in mind that the rider, after having raised the head of his mount, will entrust the horse with the task of *maintaining* this high attitude by himself through a release of his hand action. This maintenance is achieved *by the horse's muscles*, not the rider's.

This muscular process is very likely to entail an elevation of the withers, in spite of the weight of the rider. In fact, this weight makes this muscular effort somewhat more difficult for the horse — but we all know that.

This is so much so that the difference between the unmounted and the mounted horse, as concerns their answer to the elevation of the neck, will be a difference in intensity, but not in nature. And the above observation applies as well in the case of the mounted horse, namely that if the withers do not rise upon the head being lifted, the horse is afflicted with a back problem, which is amenable to chiropractic.

That Baucher felt the necessity of raising his horses' necks after he had for the most part lost the use of his legs strongly suggests there may be a connection between the two facts, namely that Baucher was seeking to obtain with the hand what the legs could no longer give. But if so, what exactly?

To answer this question, we have to challenge one of the tritest clichés of the history of horsemanship, i.e., that the rider's legs, by their pressure, provoke the engagement of the hind legs of the horse. If this were true, upon the rider using his legs by a constant pressure, a horse could literally not move forward and would remain 100% blocked at a halt, since his hind legs could not quit the engaged position supposedly created by this pressure of the rider's legs.

So what is it, if anything, that the action of the rider's legs might engage? The answer is: upon a specific conditioning (because this effect is far from being naturally granted), they may help engage the *hindquarters* (i.e., the haunches) of the horse. Although connected, engagement of the haunches and engagement of the hind legs *are two different things*, and it is very regrettable that they are so often confused in the equestrian discourse.

A horse, for instance, can engage his hind legs without engaging his hindquarters, as is the case in non-collected work (see Fig. 15). He can also engage his hindquarters without engaging his hind legs, as he does in a piaffe (see Fig. 16).

Of course, only the engagement of the hindquarters can allow the *maximum* engagement of the hind legs, as at the start of a levade (see Fig. 17), or as in all the *correctly* extended gaits in dressage.

And equally, of course, only the disengagement of the hindquarters will allow the *maximum* disengagement of the hind legs, as when a racehorse jumps out of a starting gate, or as in an incorrect

Fig. 15 - Engagement of hind legs, no engagement of hindquarters.

Fig. 16 - Engagement of hindquarters, no engagement of hind legs.

Fig. 17 - Engagement of hindquarters and engagement of hind legs.

Fig. 18 - Disengagement of hindquarters and disengagement of hind legs.

extension in dressage (see Fig. 18).

But a contradiction will appear when the object is to engage the hind legs and disengage the hindquarters or disengage the hind legs and engage the hindquarters. The contradiction is not so important in the first case [non-collected horse] (see Fig. 19a, b) as it is in the second case [collected horse] (see Fig. 20).

There is an obvious contradiction between the maintenance of the pelvis in tipped under position and the backward movement of the hind legs, and it is only when this contradiction is solved that a horse will work in a permanent collection, whatever the speed.

In his first "manner," Baucher would entrust to the rider's legs these two somewhat contradictory tasks (disengagement of the hind legs to create propulsion and engagement of the hindquarters to create balance), and one understands that there might have been

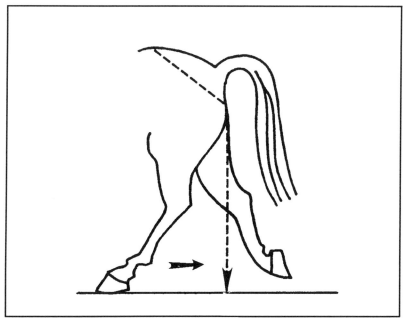

Fig. 19a - Disengagement, traction phase.

[81]

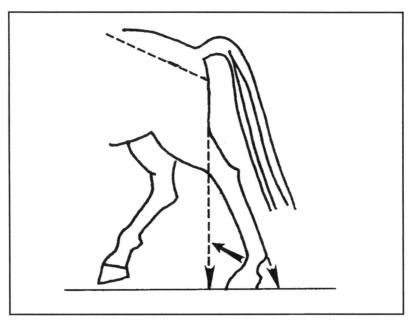

Fig. 19b - Disengagement, pushing phase; the horse backs its rear leg by flattening its croup.

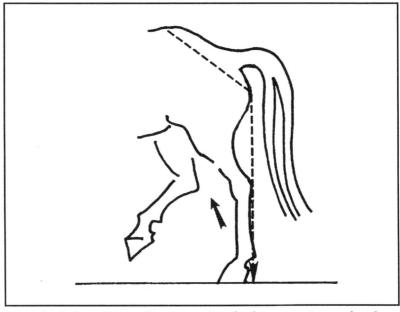

Fig. 20 - Collected horse. Tipping under of pelvis prevents rear foot from backing up. Thrust applies more vertically.

some setbacks, which I evoked in the chapter on the "effet d'ensemble."

In his second "manner," on the contrary, Baucher entrusts to the hand the task of engaging the hindquarters (through the lifting of the withers) and to the legs the task of animating the horse; that is, basically, disengaging the hind legs. The contradiction is further lessened by the use of the "hand without legs, legs without hand," and the horse attains collection sooner.

But if the contradiction is lessened, it is not totally suppressed, at least as long as the horse has not reached the "equilibrium of the first genre" of the fully trained subject. It is therefore impossible during the whole training period to separate *completely* the disengagement of the hind legs from some disengagement of the haunches, the former always entailing at least a start of the latter.

This disengagement of the haunches upon the rider's leg action is what Baucher calls "transferring weight forward, " whereas the action of hand which engages the haunches is called a "transfer of weight backwards."

This is why the impulsive action of the legs "should only transfer forward the smallest quantity of weight necessary to the movement" (cf. Faverot de Kerbrech), whereas the action of hands which transfers the weight backwards should not "take on the impulsion." In other words, the forward transfer of "weight" should not alter the balance, as its backward transfer should not alter the impulsion.

It is very obvious that this subtle-game of transferring "weight" from the hand to the legs and vice versa will be greatly facilitated by a high position of the neck.

I have placed the word "weight" in quotation marks, since I do not believe that there is much transfer of weight rearward or forward as a horse collects or stretches his frame. When a horse collects himself, front end and rear end move toward each other, obviously with very little influence, if any, on the position of the center of gravity inside the body.

I am, of course, fully aware that when a horse engages his hind legs, they bear more weight; one could call this a "transfer" of weight rearward, although it is not. But as it happens, it is precisely in the collected gaits that this engagement — thence the pseudo "transfer" of weight — is the smallest: at a collected trot, a horse does not have to overtrack, and at a piaffe, which calls for more collection than a collected trot, there is still less engagement.

Coming back to Baucher, it is obvious that he tries, with these notions of "weight" and "forces," to convey to the reader the impressions he feels on horseback: they allow him some rationality in the discourse, although their scientific value is far from overwhelming. Writes General Faverot de Kerbrech, "like all the school founders, Baucher had adopted expressions often questionable from a scientific or grammatical point of view but which it is indispensable to keep when one exposes his theories, because they bore for him a very neat and well defined meaning, and which, besides, it would be almost impossible to replace with others more becoming or more exact" (op. cit., foreword).

Let us come back to the elevation of the neck after this digression on the value of Baucher's terminology of "weight" and "forces."

As we have seen, the elevation of the neck considerably alleviates the burden of the rider's legs. In the second "manner," their role is finally reduced to giving the "go" and then remaining silent as long as there is no need for an acceleration or for specific "punctual" cues, as for a change of lead or the *start* of a passage or piaffe (I say "start" because passage and piaffe should be left to the horse and performed in the release of aids, like any other movement). One can now better assess the links of complementarity or even causality which bind together the three elements of the very "trinity" of the second "manner": the elevation of the neck, "hand without legs, legs without hand," and the "descente de jambes" (release of legs).

And what about the "mobility of the jaw" in all this? Has it been forgotten? Certainly not, and the research of Baucher in this direction indeed contributed to his decision to elevate his horse's neck. Here is why.

As his experience was growing, as his trainings were adding up, as his students were multiplying and his teachings were encountering new and unexpected problems, Baucher soon realized that he had to separate completely and carefully direct flexion of the neck from flexion of the jaw. Progressively, he came to give the latter prominence, and he stated repeatedly that flexion of the neck should be the result of yielding of the jaw and never asked for directly. Then he came to distrust even the very notion of arching the neck which so often allows the horse to dodge behind the bit, unbeknownst to his rider.

As a matter of fact, Baucher was precisely acknowledging — although implicitly — one reproach which had been made to his method in the past, namely to produce "disarticulated" necks by dint of excessive supplings.

By lifting the neck he could kill two birds with one stone: first, bring "weight" backwards; secondly, avoid any "dodging" from the demand for the mobility of the jaw. These two aspects must both be considered when one studies the notion of elevation of the neck in Baucher's second "manner," and in my opinion, the latter is perhaps more prevalent than the former. For it is not the constant and forced elevation of the head which provides balance in the Baucherist doctrine; it is the mobility of the jaw so obtained. If, after having obtained it with a high position of head, the rider is lucky enough to keep it unaltered as the head comes back to a more average — and sometimes even rather low — set, he or she will find that the balance as well has been kept unaltered.

Another proceeding, very little publicized and even usually overlooked by those who abide by the second "manner," can confirm this point of view: I am speaking of the "ramener outré" — an exaggerated overbending of the neck.

In the "ramener outré," the horse's muzzle is brought to literally touch the chest, and the flexion of the jaw is asked for in this position. Visibly, the purpose is the same as with the maximum elevation of the head: apply directly to the mouth in denying the horse any possibility of using his neck as a "bumper." In the elevation of the head, the goal is fulfilled by extending (unfurling) the neck; in the "ramener outré," this "bumper capability" of the neck is, as it were, "saturated," the neck being given all the curvature it can take.

The "ramener outré" is a very little known aspect of the second "manner," since the cliché has it that Baucher would overbend his horses' necks in his first "manner" (which would probably happen at times but was not the purpose of the method) and would, on the contrary, elevate them in his second "manner."

To my knowledge, the "ramener outré" appears only in General de Kerbrech's work and not in the written work of Baucher, although we are made to presume that it was in the last oral teachings of Baucher, since General de Kerbrech's book has for its base the notes he took daily of the lessons and conversations he had with his Master.

It is interesting to notice that, whereas the elevation of the neck is scattered in a few paragraphs throughout the book, the "ramener outré" gives rise to a full chapter by the end of it. To put this proceeding into a correct perspective, I shall quote the first two sentences and the last sentence of this chapter.

Beginning of chapter: "The ramener 'outré' is but a *means* to fix the head in a normal ramener through a *momentary* exaggeration of the exigencies of the rider. One should use it only if one wants to carry out the schooling until the *total* annihilation of the resistances which the mouth and the neck may present in any position, regardless of the gait."

End of chapter: *"The elevation of the neck compounded with the 'ramener outré' gives and fixes the true head set,* which thenceforth will never ever be lost, either in the active gaits or in the difficult movements."

To bring this presentation of the second "manner" to a close, we have yet to describe two more proceedings: the "descente de main et de jambes" (release of hand and legs) and the "separation of force from movement."

The "descente de main" (release of the hand) was introduced by La Guérinière in **Ecole de Cavalerie** (1731). It amounted to leaving the horse absolutely free from any support of the hand (that is, any contact with the bit), *after having set him on the haunches.*

The "descente de jambes" (release of the legs) is introduced by Baucher in the 12th edition of his method in 1864. It amounts to leaving the horse with the task of maintaining the position and the action, that is, the movement, the legs intervening only to start or restore it. Even the regularity of the movement (i.e., its cadence), is left to the horse, *as it should proceed from his unaltered equilibrium.*

General de Kerbrech constantly insists on the necessity of dispensing with the legs or the hand or both as soon and as thoroughly as possible. One may be more systematic and posit as a principle of training that *an aid must quit as soon as its purpose has been fulfilled*. The aids start, restore, transform; they never maintain.

As for the "separation of force from movement," it consists of stopping and relaxing the horse as soon as a resistance occurs. But this relaxation is not limited to the demand for a yielding of the jaw; it is furthered by a period of *total inactivity* which can last several minutes if necessary. The rider *does not allow the horse to depart from his lightness* at any time; if the lightness is lost, he does not try to restore it *within the movement*, that is, in motion; he stops and relaxes the horse as described above. The period of rest is meant to calm the horse so that the previous movement does not resound, reverberate, or vibrate any more in his body and mind.

Baucher insists a great deal on observing this principle; he promises wonders out of it. "These moments of rest, repeated with this scrupulous care, bring about results which will amaze the rider" (op. cit., p. 208).

As we see, although with new means, Baucher remains faithful to his philosophy of yore: introduce the movement as with an eyedropper.

---

[1] Vertebral blockings—due to local muscular spasms—are very frequent and should be taken care of by a chiropractor or, better, an equine osteopath. Any vertebral blocking, more so from C1 (Atlas, next to the skull) to T15 (under the saddle), may hamper the uplifting of the whole spinal column.

Even a subluxation in a "sacro-iliac" joint (pelvis) may come as a hindrance for this result.

Chapter 7

Légèreté vs. Durchlässigkeit

T he Polish Captain Zdzislaw Baranowski did a great service to the world riding community when, in 1955, he had his **International Horseman's Dictionary** published.

This dictionary is in three languages: German, English, and French. When glancing through it, I made an interesting discovery, namely that there is no equivalent for the French *légèreté* (lightness) in the German riding terminology, but at the same time, there is no French equivalent for the German *Durchlässigkeit* (permeability).

This semantic phenomenon is, I think, highly descriptive of two different riding styles, and I intend to elaborate on it. But first, we have to give clear *and technical* definitions of these two terms.

Although they were taken from two widely acknowledged authorities (General Decarpentry for the French, Waldemar Seunig for the German), the definitions offered by Captain Baranowski's dictionary are not precise enough. *Légèreté* is described in this way: "parfaite obéissance du cheval aux plus légères indications de la main et des talons du cavalier," which translates as "perfect obedience from the horse to the slightest indications of the rider's hand and heels."

This definition is insufficient, since it does not take into consideration the absence of *"appui"* (leaning onto the bit) that the notion of "légèreté" implies. A horse may perfectly lean (understood in a mellow way) onto his bit and nevertheless yield to a slight *addition* of weight in the rider's hand — and then he displays *Durchlässigkeit* (permeability).

This latter term, in turn, is not quite properly described in the **Dictionary**. The definition reads "Fähigkeit und Bereitschaft des Pferdes auf die Hilfen einzugehen," which I shall allow myself to translate as "aptitude and readiness of the horse to respond to the aids." This does not take into account the notion of (figurative) "penetration" of the aids through the body of the horse which is implied in "Durchlässigkeit."

Surprisingly, the French wording related to this typically German concept in the dictionary is quite satisfactory. It reads "aptitude du cheval à laisser passer à travers lui les aides du cavalier," that is, "aptitude of the horse to let pass through his body the aids of the rider." We will accept this definition.

As for "légèreté," I would like to propose this description I excerpt from Gen. Faverot de Kerbrech's book **Dressage Methodique du Cheval de Selle** (translation is mine): "Lightness is recognized by the lack of resistance to the effects of the curb or snaffle; the half-tension of one rein or both must bring about the mellow mobility of the lower jaw without the head moving and without the opening of the jaw being noticeably apparent, and the tongue of the horse must make the bits jingle against each other, which sometimes produces a silver-toned ringing; let us further add that this mellow mobility must last for a certain time and not stop abruptly.

"Such is the set of conditions which constitutes true lightness. This latter is, for the rider, the revealing and infallible sign of the perfect equilibrium of his horse, as long as it remains unaltered.

"...Each time that, on foot or on horseback, the rider intends to ask whatever from the horse he is training, he must begin with making him light, that is, look for the mellow mobility of the jaw" (op. cit. pp. 7 and 8).

This amounts to the sheer destruction of the "appui" (support given by the rider and taken by the horse onto the bit - cf. La Guérinière, **Ecole de Cavalerie**) and its replacement by a mere "contact," whose magnitude, in any case, must remain under the threshold of the "half-tension" of the reins.

One will notice that General de Kerbrech does not evoke the lightness to the legs, since it comes mandatorily as a consequence of the state of balance created *ipso facto* by the relaxation of the jaw.

With this conception, when a horse is fully trained (and this, of course, will take some time), he is always in a perfect state of balance, since imbalance would result in contractions, immediately felt and destroyed by the rider's hand. So there is almost *no more use of the aids*; they intervene *only for transitions*, or to start or restore a movement, never to *actively maintain it* (whereas "appui" is a constant, even if unobtrusive, intervention of the rider's hand in the *maintenance* of his horse's balance).

According to this theory (and practice), from piaffe to extended trot, a horse *keeps practically the same balance*, which is realized by a constant engagement of the haunches, that is, a forward "locking" of his pelvic bone, a constant elevation of his withers.

Extension is no longer the opposite of collection; it is simply the *expression of collection in speed* and, as such, can only be asked for *at an advanced stage of the training*. Another consequence of this conception is that half-halts do not apply anymore. They were just a means to train a horse; they do not remain a means to ride a fully trained horse.

In the other (German) type of horsemanship, the half-halt *is a staple*, since the development of a gait accepts, nay, calls for, a progressive alteration of the balance toward the shoulders as it extends and back toward the haunches as it "collects."

This style requires a horse who remains *faithfully* (although smoothly) *on the bit* in the upward transitions and displays *permeability* in the downward transitions.

This conception is evident in the choice of the terms used to describe the development of a gait, the trot for instance, which will include "collected" trot and then working, medium, and extended trot. The notion of collection affects only the slowest aspect of the gait. If the other conception had prevailed in the FEI, the sequence would have read: slow, medium, extended trot, it being well understood that collection presides over all stages of this development. This, however, will not be easily understood or accepted by many a rider, since the notion of collection, in most people's mind, is indelibly linked to the shrinking of the gaits, not their development. We tend to think that a horse who is collected will never fully express his impulsion in the forward movement. We tend to consider collection a constraint, whereas it is, as a matter of fact, a liberation.

Let me remind the reader of how this can be upheld.

All proceeds from the absence, in the horse's skeleton, of a collar bone. The spine and rib cage of the horse, which "float" between the shoulder blades, to which they are attached only by means of muscles and ligaments, will at first knuckle under the rider's weight, which will result in a noticeable stress likely to seriously impair the horse's balance. He who was so graceful in liberty will suddenly become clumsy under the saddle.

It is an observation of long standing that the relaxation of the jaw greatly helps in fighting these abnormal contractions and in so doing helps in restoring the natural balance of a horse. A possible physiological explanation of the phenomenon was given to me recently by Nancy Nicholson, a biologist at Miami University in Oxford, OH, (and a dressage rider). I give here her interesting explanation.

Writes Mrs. Nicholson: "The relaxed jaw allows the geniohyoid muscle at the base of the tongue in which is embedded the front projection of the hyoid apparatus (which is in turn connected at its lower back end to the sternum) to respond to the most refined dialogue between bit and tongue. Under these conditions, the rider is able to give himself to the horse, who is in self-carriage."

With respect to this question of the relaxation of the lower jaw, the riding world is divided into two camps, equally ignorant: those who reject it viscerally and without further test because they think that it sets the horse "behind the bit" (an expression which has done more harm than good to horsemanship) and those who believe in it because their horses have taught them how powerful a purveyor of balance it can be, but have no understanding of how and why it works. It is obvious that serious scientific studies should be made in order to bring more light to the matter and by the same token help solve this sterile confrontation.

Be that as it may, the combination of the relaxation of the lower jaw with a progressive and reasonable elevation of the neck will literally *lock* the pelvis in a tipped-under position, assuring a *constant engagement of the haunches*, regardless of the speed.

This position, which is the essence of collection, restores the balance but in the beginning limits the possibilities of forward movement, since it gives precedence to the *traction* phase of the hind legs (which happens during the time the hooves are situated under the horse's mass) over the *pushing* phase (which occurs as soon as the hooves pass behind the mass). With most horses (save for the Andalusians, Lusitanos, and Lipizzans), this entails a whole re-education of the locomotion process, which normally tends to rely more on the pushing phase, hence requiring at least a partial disengagement of the hindquarters (flattening of the croup).

Before going any further in our theoretical explanations, let us observe here that most German horses display a flat croup. This is due to the high degree of Arabian blood which runs in their veins, since the ennoblement of the local carriage breeds was sought more through infusion of Arabian blood than through crossing with English Thoroughbreds. This is consistent with their breeders' riding goals, which aim at developing sheer thrust, so they are therefore obliged to equate collection to shrinking of the gaits.

Thus we are in the presence of two markedly different conceptions as concerns the balance of a horse. With the first conception (lightness), a horse should be constantly *collected*, even in an upward transition; with the second (permeability), he should be constantly *collectable*, for a downward transition.

This difference reflects somewhat the psychological gap which separates the French from the Germans. The French are overly fond of security, of stability, so they will not try to "get at fast gaits what they cannot get at slow gaits" (Baucher). The Germans prefer movement over stability. So they will choose to "work the movement by the movement," to use another expression of Baucher's.

The French like elegance, even in the technical field. To painstakingly fashion a horse by dint of numerous and fastidious sessions of working trot is of very little appeal to them, whereas establishing at once a balance from which *all* will proceed is for them much more exciting. Besides, it is "satisfying for the mind," which is of great importance for a Frenchman.

Germans dislike all that is static: they *need* movement (perhaps because of some inner feeling of insecurity, which also would make them aggressive). In the choice constantly proposed to the rider by the practice of horsemanship, between thrust and lightness, they will certainly choose thrust. The need for pushing is innate to them: everybody knows how "pushy" they can be in business. The notion of "Drang" (push, momentum) is more prevalent in their cultural and political life than in any other nation's: "Sturm und Drang" (Storm and Stress) of the Literary Romanticism of the late Eighteenth Century, "Drang nach Osten" (Thrust Eastward) of Pan-Germanism.

An acquaintance of mine once defined—excellently in my view—the French style of riding as "feminine." By contrast, I would say that German riding is certainly masculine, virile, hence the stress borne upon forward thrust. I won't elaborate further, lest I become too Freudian.

This distrust for all that is static is further demonstrated by the existence, in the German language, of two different verbs to translate "to be": "sein," which is static, and "werden," which is dynamic (to become, to turn to). Things never "are" for the German mentality: they become.

In his preface to the French translation of Steinbrecht's **Gymnasium of the Horse**, General Decarpentry writes (translation is mine):

"Whereas with us, stubborn 'carvers,' shoulder-in has become a particular exercise, distinct in its goal and means from those which precede and follow it, it is, for our neighbors, but one of the thousands of stills of a flowing movie, one moment in the uninterrupted

[95]

progression of an ongoing suppling work of the spine, started on one only and at first rectilinear track then curved and continued on two tracks up to the pirouette on the haunches inclusively."

How true! And just as Wagner's music is nothing else than a constant *metamorphosis* of an obsessive theme (the "Leitmotif"), Steinbrecht's riding seems to me a constant metamorphosis of the same theme of the unending, unsolvable, and crucifying contradiction between the needs of costal flexion and the fundamental, visceral desire for forward movement.

Let's now get back to the technical brass tacks. If the ever-collected horse displaying *légèreté* requires the mobility of the jaw, the ever-collectable horse displaying *Durchlässigkeit* requires "appui."

"Appui" is not very easy to describe, since (like "légèreté," as a matter of fact) it is about a feeling. La Guérinière gives of it the following definition: "...the feeling produced by the action of the bridle in the rider's hand, and conversely the action that the rider's hand operates upon the bars of the horse's mouth" (**Ecole de Cavalerie**, 1769 edition, p. 131). The translation is mine; it is practically the same as the one on page 16 of the translation of Part Two of **Ecole de Cavalerie** published by Xenophon Press. But in my opinion, this latter commits the error of translating "appui" as "contact." Now "contact," for the **Webster's New Collegiate Dictionary**, is a "union," an "apparent touching or mutual tangency, " a "junction," an "association," a "connection," a "relationship," etc...all words which *do not at all imply any notion of "weight" or "pressure."* Unfortunately, that's what it's all about. Probably "support" would be the English term closest to the French "appui."

In this respect, the reading of **The International Horseman's Dictionary** is more explicit, at least in its German part. It indeed establishes a distinction between (1) *der Kontakt* (erste Fühlungsnahme des Reiters mit dem Pferdemaul, in English "first contact felt by the rider with the horse's mouth") and (2) *die Anlehnung des Pferdes* ("the leaning of the horse onto his bit"). (Translations are mine.)

Thus, in German riding (as well as in the "d'Aurisme" in France), the rider's hand alone establishes a first "contact" by adjusting the reins, whereupon the rider's legs, by pushing the horse forward, have to create the "appui."

It is too often assumed that the increased tension with the reins results from the engagement of the hindquarters brought about by the action of the rider's legs. But the purpose of the engagement of the hindquarters is to alleviate the front end of the horse, thus the tension in the rein should be *lessened*, not augmented.

This leads us to three conclusions:

1) "Appui" is always the share of imbalance, since it is the negation of self-carriage. Would the horse be abruptly denied the "appui," he would lose his balance or would have to immediately take in charge the part of the balance he was heretofore entrusting his rider with. In other words, when a horse takes a support from his rider's hand, he more or less is using his rider's muscles instead of his.

2) "Appui" should thus be considered at best a necessary evil; it should therefore go fading out as the training progresses. Hence there should be *in fine* no difference between the "Latin" and the "Teutonic" schools.

3) The truth is that when, upon the action of the rider's legs, the contact is reinforced and transformed into an "appui," it is precisely because the horse has extended his frame, that is, dimin-

ished his degree of collection by somewhat flattening his croup, extending his neck, and opening the angle of his poll.

Although it has to be opposed if we want to foster collection, this phenomenon of opening the frame when urged to move forward is absolutely natural with the horse.

The "appui" thus created can be utilized in three different ways:

1) The rider accepts it passively, which means that although not accepting the resistances of force (horse's pulling), he/she will accept the resistances of "weight" (horse's bearing). Therefore, he/she will have to resort to the half-halt (a re-equilibration from front to rear) each time he/she has to perform any movement requiring collection.

2) The rider, by his/her own resistance, uses this increase in contact to obtain a flexion of the lower jaw which, in turn, fosters collection. This is the "effet d'ensemble" of Baucher in his first manner.

3) The rider will make use of it in a very subtle way to literally bend at will the horse to the degree of collection required by such or such exercise in a sort of permanent and deftly modulated half-halt.

This calls for a quick analysis.

Any bending of a horse concerns two sets of muscles: on the one hand, those which create the bending, which work in contraction; on the other hand, the antagonistic muscles, which tend to limit the bending. They work in elongation...up to a point (i.e., they resist).

The "appui" always matches the resistance of the antagonistic system.

In the hypothesis we are studying, the rider seeks the schooling of this set of antagonistic muscles so that they yield if he/she acts, resist if he/she resists, and act if he yields.

In this way, the horse may be compared to a bow and the

"appui" to the modulated traction of the archer's hand.

Needless to say, this perfection is probably very rarely attained.

I now have to come back to the consideration by which I assumed that *in fine* horsemanship the "Latin" and "Teutonic" traditions should converge, since "self-carriage"is the name of the game.

A few days after *Kronos,* ridden for Germany by Lt. Heinz Pollay, won the Dressage Gold Medal in the Olympic Games at Berlin in 1936, Cmdt. Xavier Lesage, who four years earlier won for France the Olympic Games in Los Angeles, was invited to ride *"impromptu"* the said *Kronos* in the presence of a small, but select, attendance. At first he felt a little out of place on this horse who had been trained according to another school, but soon he overcame this feeling and achieved a very brilliant performance, which allowed him to testify "that at this time, there was no noticeable difference between the French and the German schools, at least as concerns Kronos ."

And indeed, there is on page 98 of **Buchers Geschichte des Pferdesports** (by Max Amman) an impressive photograph of *Kronos* and Lt. Pollay at a showcase piaffe, which gives a great impression of correctness, classicism, and... lightness!

Now I don't want to offend anybody, but this quality of piaffe we don't see any more in dressage arenas, even at the highest level. How come?

I have an answer, and I take full responsibility for it: "appui" is probably the culprit.

Dressage riders nowadays are too much "hooked" on the reins, and subsequently their horses are too low in front and to "enclosed." This often produces piaffes where the front legs go back as the hind legs engage (like in the worst of Baucher first "manner"). At best, there sometimes is some activity behind, but the front leg gesture lacks completely in liveliness.

Now is this compatible with the description, by Steinbrecht, of the "ideal piaffe"?:

"In the absolutely ideal piaffe, the horse raises its foreleg so high that the forearm is horizontal and it raises the hind leg to the point that its hoof reaches half the height of the splint bone hollow of the resting leg, with the body performing only a soft, yet strong up and down movement. *Every step the horse must chew on the bit* (I italicized), with its neck well elevated and its poll yielding." (**Gymnasium of the Horse**, translated by Helen K. Gibble, Xenophon Press, 1995, pp. 255-56).

It seems to me very significant that Steinbrecht, in this description of a brilliant piaffe, mentions that the jaw should yield by each step, as if it were a condition for this perfection.

Baucher was much reproached for putting double bridles on young horses and seeking too soon the flexion of the jaw. Count d'Aure, the principal enemy of Baucher, wrote: "The best preparation to train a young horse is to accustom him to proceed forward while pulling onto his bridoons". As for the 1912 **Manuel d'Equitation et de Dressage (Manual of Horsemanship and Training)** of the French Army, although pretty much impregnated with Baucherist principles, it states that, before looking for the lightness of the jaw, the rider "by the mellow fixity of his hand, will endeavor to obtain a trusting 'appui' in the position — even if incorrect — which is more familiar to the horse" (op.cit. p.76, translation is mine).

Many a reader will probably object that one should not be lax about the position of head for the sheer sake of "appui." But let it be reminded here that the "ramener" in the French school had to proceed from the direct flexion of the jaw, which was to be the next step.

Be that as it may, in the United States, where to have a horse, even a young horse, "above the bit" is considered a mortal sin, the question does not arise, as it seems that for a great number to place a horse's head low and "tucked in" is the alpha and omega of the whole horsemanship. Thus is the horse "pretty." Let's take a photograph. And, of course, we'd better limit it to the head and neck, since we have no guarantee that the rear end is going to be as "pretty."

Wise prudence, since as a matter of fact, we are almost guaranteed that the rear end *won't* be engaged, because this too low and tucked in position of the head *prevents it from being so.* Few horses indeed have enough suppleness in their lumbar and sacral areas to allow the pelvis to tip under if the withers are collapsed.

Now, although it is possible, through a skillful use of the spurs, to artificially lift the withers area of a horse whose neck and head are low, this depressed position of the front end is most likely to entail a collapsing of the withers area, as we have seen.

So much so that, by focussing too soon on a too low and too bent head set, the rider literally locks out the rear end and seriously jeopardizes the chances of success of the so-famed work "from rear to front." Sure enough, the progressive engagement of the rear end should alleviate the front end, but alas, the door is locked, and *by the rider's hand to boot!*

This, in my opinion, accounts for the poor quality of the piaffes one can see in this day and age, a misfortune which strikes even the greatest.

If it were only about piaffe, the damage would be limited, since it does not imply so many horses. But the same wrong conception handicaps thousands of devoted average riders. They are in the rut: they cannot extend, cannot go laterally, cannot back up, for lack of balance, that is, for lack of a proper "tipping under" of the pelvis. They can pass down transitions which may deceive the onlooker by their militaristic "energy" but are suggestive rather of the heavy truck using its Westinghouse brakes, with the same diving movement in front.

Coming back to the gist of this chapter, to wit, "Légèreté vs. Durchlässigkeit," we are in the presence of two different approaches using two different tools. The first—lightness—wants a constantly collected horse and for this uses the mobility of the jaw. The other, fostering "appui", looks for a constantly collectable horse. The point I want to make is that appui, by fostering a low and tucked in position of the head, is less likely to lead to real collection, that is, to a thorough and permanent engagement of the hindquarters.

Therefore, even for those who want to stick to the philosophy of "appui," because they believe (wrongly, in my opinion) that the mobility of the lower jaw will set their horses "behind the bit," I would give this piece of advise: do not look for the "ramener" (classical head set) before having raised the withers. In other words, rather than lowering the end part of the neck, raise its base.

How to achieve this will be discussed in the next chapter.

Chapter 8

Lifting the Withers

Training a horse consists of developing his power and in the meantime developing the ways to check this very power. Except for race training, this second aspect is by far the most important.

As far as dressage is concerned, this is even its essence. Why do we school a horse to better respond to the aids, why do we supple him, if not to tame his power in order to make him as mobile as possible?

Mobility is indeed the name of the game. A horse is mobile if he can stop, spin, move sideways, and surge forward (which implies acceleration rather than sheer speed), all movements which were useful, nay, vital, at war at a time when men would fight on horseback.

This explains the necessity of collection. Collection is nothing else than the attitude which allows a horse the maximum mobility.

Some will probably object that when in liberty, a horse doesn't have to be collected and nevertheless may prance in the most astounding way. So why not trust the horse's innate feeling of balance and leave him alone?

This surely seems very wise. Unfortunately, as soon as he is ridden, a horse loses this blessed easiness; his balance—if the rider leaves him alone—will no longer be the balance he has in liberty. This should suffice to justify collection, let alone the fact that, when ridden, the horse will be called on to do *more difficult* figures than those he would have done in liberty, and do them when we want it and not when he does.

Still, it is very instructive to observe a horse moving on his own in the pasture. At liberty, whenever a horse wants to pass in no time from gallop to a halt, what strikes the onlooker is the spectacular tipping under of his pelvis. The ancient Masters would call this gesture "falquer des hanches" ("fold in the haunches"). It seems to be the *sine qua non* condition for an increased balance, that is, the best possible check for the "kinetic energy," i.e., the momentum.

Necessary in liberty, this strong "bascule" of the pelvis is, of course, still more necessary under the rider's weight.

This "tipping under" of the pelvis is allowed on the one hand by the play of the sacro-iliac joints, on the other hand by the suppleness of the lumbar segment.

However, the sacro-iliac joints as well as the lumbar-vertebral joints have a limited range of flexion. Therefore, a horse will have to rise the other extremity of his spinal column in order to alleviate the tension brought upon these areas. And this we know he can do, thanks to the absence of a solid connection between his withers and his shoulder blades.

So the spinal column of the horse will modify its angle with respect to the horizontal line. In the equestrian literature, this phenomenon is called "lowering of the croup;" "tipping under" of the croup would probably be more appropriate. The aspect of "lowering" was more prevalent in the baroque era, when the school leaps — or "airs above the ground" — were an important part of the riding program. Any leap requires a prior bending of the hocks, and yes, this bending lowers the whole of the rear end. I shall come back to this consideration later.

It has been sometimes debated whether the elevation of the front end is a cause or a consequence of the lowering of the croup, but this debate is futile, since the horse is a whole: these two movements are linked to each other. Yet one can affirm that if, for any reason, the withers cannot rise, then the horse's engagement possibilities will be drastically limited.

At this point, we have a clearer picture of what collection is: a shrinking of the medial line of the horse (edge of shoulder to edge of buttocks) which lifts the withers, tips the pelvis under, and allows a horse to deeply engage his hind legs if the movement so requires.

This contraction of the horse's body is twice beneficial for his balance: on the one hand by the possibilities it offers of engagement of the hind legs (tipping under of the pelvis), on the other hand by its counterbalancing the crushing effect of the rider's weight (lifting of the withers area).

This picture, however, applies more particularly for a horse at a halt (piaffe) or at a canter, because in these two cases, the horse engages *both hind legs together*, or almost so. At a walk or trot, it has to be noticed that the deep engagement of one hind leg does not have any effect on the "tipping under" of the pelvis, because when one hind leg engages, the other disengages, and the "tipping under" influence of the engagement on one side of the haunches is neutral-ized by the "flattening" influence of the disengagement on the other side.

This shows, incidentally, that pushing a horse at a trot in order to make him track up has very little to do with collection. When a horse, at a trot or walk, engages deeply but one *leg*, i.e., the forward moving hind leg, he does not work toward collection; he is just making big steps.

He can make big steps — or short steps — regardless of his degree of collection. The degree of collection of a horse is thus measured by the magnitude of the "tucking in" of his buttocks. And since tucking the pelvis in is synonymous with raising the withers, one can also state that the elevation of the withers gives the measure of collection. This is a very important conclusion.

Surprisingly, this notion of lifting of the withers is practically absent in the works of the great Masters, although they mention the "alleviation of the front end," which is rather vague. Besides, collection does not offer a rigid, stereotyped model, since each epoch has had its own type of collection, justified by a particular purpose.

In the baroque era, when school leaps were extensively practiced, the flexion of the hind joints of the horse was the main feature of collection. Here, I have to mention a little known anatomical mechanism, a muscular set-up which links the stifle to the hock, acting like a "pantograph," so that these two joints are bound to bend or unbend together; when the stifle bends, so does the hock and vice versa. This fact makes it obvious that the bending of the hock is most likely to happen when the leg is placed vertically under the mass. When the leg is engaged, the stifle is open, and so is the hock. If then the ensemble stifle/hock would bend, the horse would do a levade or a pesade (or fall).

When hock and stifle bend, the coxo-femoral joint (the buttock joint) is not bound to act in like manner, but if ever this would happen, then the bending process of the whole hindquarters would have a crushing effect, the edge of buttock would *back up*, and the croup would *flatten*. Collection of the Ancient School was not completely exempt from this danger, and I will remind the reader here that the Baucherists would compare a horse collected in the ancient way to a cat about to jump on the table.

Conversely, the supporters of the Old System would compare "Baucherized" horses to cats who round their backs. The practice of the "effet d'ensemble" would indeed foster the flexion of the spine *right in its middle,* under the saddle (thoracic vertebrae T12 and T13). Rather than rising, the withers would "fan out" (which, anatomically, is a good thing), entailing some lowering of the neck. Front legs and hind legs would go toward each other, the shoulders coming into an overhanging position with respect to the front feet. This is about the celebrated position of the "buck on a peak."

So there does not seem to be much elevation of the withers in the two examples above, the old system and Baucherism in its first "manner."

Still, one should not judge a system of horsemanship by its excesses. When it is not about "airs above the ground," the illustrations of **Ecole de Cavalerie** (La Guérinière, 1731) show horses whose rear ends are well tucked under, and whose withers rise marvelously.

As for the attitude of the "buck on a peak" of Baucher's horses in his first "manner," one should bear in mind that it was about an exercise meant to increase momentarily, and for schooling purposes, the exigencies of collection. When the matter was to perform a movement, the rider would allow some opening of this over-collected frame, and the horse would take a more natural position. Baucher, in his first "manner," and only as a result of a schooling from horseback (the work in hand was developed mostly with the second "manner"), would obtain from his horses the horizontal extension of one front limb at will, and I don't see this happening without a notable elevation of the withers.

So in both cases, elevation of the withers would happen in fact but is not focussed on in the theoretical explanations.

Steinbrecht (1808-1885), who is often cited as a reference for modern dressage, acknowledges only one way to "alleviate the front end," i.e., progressively engage the hind legs under the horse's body. As for the progressive lifting of the neck, which he also practices, he bestows only one purpose upon it: bringing about the flexion of the hocks. He reasons exactly as if there were a "peg" in the horse's shoulders around which the spine rotates, so that when the head rises, the haunches will lower, which they can only do through a bending of the hocks.

"The cervical vertebrae together with the dorsal vertebrae constitute a two-armed lever which has the forelegs as its fulcrum; the raising of one of the lever arms has a lowering effect on the other and vice-versa" (**Gymnasium of the Horse**, translated by Helen K. Gibble, Xenophon Press, 1995, p. 115).

General Decarpentry does not agree with this reasoning, arguing that a horse has no clavicle, and that therefore there is no "fulcrum" between the cervical part and the thoracic part of the vertebral column.

"The spine of the horse, through the intermediary of the thorax to which it is joined, lies between the two shoulders in a kind of cradle constituted of muscles and cartilage. This cradle is neither rigid, or of a fixed shape; it has the elasticity common to all muscular tissue. It can stretch downward and thereby allow the thorax, and therefore the spine, to descend by taking advantage of the elasticity of its cradle.

"If one lifts the neck, its lower part sinks into the cradle, the withers sink between the shoulders, and the spine, behind the withers, sinks under the saddle" (**Academic Equitation**, translation by

[108]

Nicole Bartle, J. A. Allen & Co. Ltd.,London, p. 73).

There is a big flaw in General Decarpentry's reasoning, namely that if the withers can sink, they by the same token can rise (as a matter of fact, there is a muscle for this, the "serratus thoracis;" it is fixed at its lower part on the first eight or nine ribs and at its higher part onto the upper inside part of the shoulder blade).

And since, yes, the spine is rather rigid, the fulcrum—if fulcrum there be—is to be looked for in the rear of the said spine, that is, by the coxo-femoral joint. Thus the lever it is about is not a two arm lever but simply a classical lever of the first "genre," where the resistance (weight of the rider) is situated between the fulcrum and the acting force (serratus thoracis). See Figure 21.

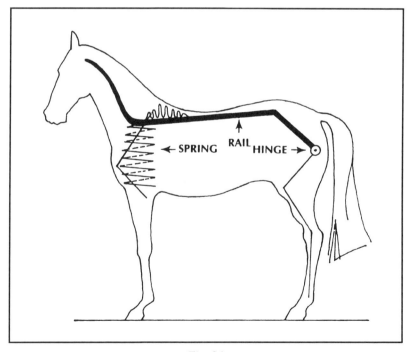

Fig. 21

This flaw in General Decarpentry's reasoning triggered off my reflexion on the matter (some thirty years ago). I knew for a fact that lifting the neck, regardless of any previous bending at the poll, would elevate the withers and hence the whole back of the horse (or was I the only rider on earth whose horses would react in this way?). About the same time, I noticed that a horse who had come to my barn the previous year sizing up 15.1-^{1}/$_2$ hh. was now sizing 15.3 hh.

This one and a half inch difference could not be explained through biological growth (growth of the bones) given the age of the horse. The only explanation was that the exercising had toned his withers area in such a way that the spine had been permanently lifted.

Then I thought that probably the size of an unmounted horse would differ from the size of the same horse under the rider's weight. I experimented and found out that all my horses were shrinking an average ^{2}/$_3$ in. under 150 pounds of weight. One of them was even losing 1-^{1}/$_2$ in. Interestingly enough, this horse was an inveterate "puller."

Subsequently, I focused more and more on this phenomenon of the lifting of the withers, up to making it the base of my understanding of academic horsemanship, that is, collected horsemanship.

As an admirer of Baucher, more particularly in his second "manner," I would have liked to be able to say that the French Master, by the end of his quest, had become aware of this aspect of the functioning of the equine machine, but unfortunately, I can't: nothing in the Baucherists' documents allows one to think so.

But we should notice that if Baucher had not got clear enough a consciousness of the phenomenon in his theoretical reasoning, he had at least acknowledged it *de facto*, since the exercises of the second "manner" are certainly the more advisable to achieve that goal.

As for the German School, at least in its modern expression, I stated in the previous chapter that its focusing too much on "appui," that is, on a rather strong contact with the bit, was at risk of setting the head in too low a position, therefore endangering the sitting on the haunches, without which there are no real High School movements.

It seems that some of its representatives share my concerns, as stands out from this quote from Baron von Blixen-Finecke of Sweden, which I excerpt from **The Natural Rider**, a book by Mary Wanless (Simon and Schuster Publishers):

"We all want lightness of the forehand. In order to achieve it we work on more engagement of the hind legs. *I invite people to think the other way round: work on lightness and submission of the forehand; the hind legs will engage as soon as there is room for them*" (italics are mine).

Interestingly enough, Baron von Blixen-Finecke was first and foremost an outside rider. He won the Gold medal in eventing in Helsinki in 1952.

And now, let's come to a few exercises I think most appropriate to achieve the elevation of the withers.

A preliminary remark: before starting these exercises, you must check that the withers area of your horse is free from any subluxation, any "locking." It can be done in this way: with the point of a hoof peak, push upward on the sternum at about 6-8 in. from the front legs. The withers must noticeably rise (1 to $1\text{-}^1/2$ in.).

If the withers do not rise, or do it in a questionable way, chances are that one or several vertebrae of this area are "locked," that is, withheld in a given position by a local muscular spasm. A subluxation of the thoracic vertebrae situated immediately after the withers area

(T9 to T13) may also be involved. In any case, see a chiropractor, or, better, an osteopath.

It may nevertheless happen that the horse's withers don't rise correctly, if at all, under the rider's weight, although they yielded markedly upon an upward pressure applied on the sternum. In this case, one will observe that the upward movement of the withers is more conspicuous in their rear part than in front. This reveals a probable subluxation with the very first thoracic vertebrae (Tl, T2, T3).[1] A chiropractor can help you with that as well. The rule in this matter is that, as long as the withers don't rise *without any hollowing of the back* when the horse's head is lifted from the ground, there is need for some chiropractic or, better, osteopathic[2] intervention.

To raise the head from the ground, the rider faces the horse, places his thumbs in the rings of the snaffle, and pushes in the direction of the poll.

Use of the spurs at a halt

A) Halt. Ask for a flexion of jaw (the horse must *let go of the bit*). When this is completed, apply progressively and eventually firmly the spurs near to the girth as possible.[3] You will feel a noticeable elevation of the spine in front of the saddle. This will also confirm the quality of your horse's head set.

B) At a halt, lift the head to a suitable maximum (the highest your horse can give, head horizontal, or near the horizontal). Ask for a yielding of the jaw (mobility of the tongue). When you get it, immediately lengthen your reins,[4] lower your hands into a regular position, calmly apply the spurs as near to the girth as possible, *and push the horse forward one step*. Practicing these exercises often will give tone to the concerned area.

Turning around the shoulders

This will surprise more than one person, since this exercise is often presented as setting a horse on the shoulders. It is easy to demonstrate that this is not so. In order to be on the shoulders, a horse has to lengthen his base of support by flattening his croup and moving his hind legs back. In a turning around the shoulders, on the contrary, the horse has to engage his inside hind leg rather deeply; crossing over is a painful gymnastic for a horse, so it is ludicrous to think that, in order to move his croup circularly around his shoulders, a horse will favor the lateral component of the movement over the longitudinal.

It is precisely this push of the rear against a front end that resists which brings about collection. But this opposition, instead of being headlong, is slanted, like in a shoulder-in, and here lies the advantage of this exercise. Like in a shoulder-in, the horse is worked one haunch at a time. Like in a shoulder-in, checking the outside shoulder to prevent it from "falling" out is important.

To begin with, one will use hand and leg on the same side, the horse turning his haunches in the direction opposite to his bending.

This bending should be very limited from the onset, since it will be progressively reversed to transform the movement little by little into a "reversed pirouette," in which the horse "sees his haunch coming."

The horse should pivot around his inside front foot (case of a simple turning around shoulders) or outside front foot (reversed pirouette), that is, pivot around the right front foot if the croup is moving to left and vice versa.

A departure into canter (with the inside leg) upon completion of a reversed pirouette is a very useful movement.

This exercise also perfects the "ramener" (head set).

To make a horse better understand in the beginning, it may be advisable to work him from the ground. The rider faces the horse, walking slowly backward on a small circle, using the dressage whip to gently invite the croup to describe a wider circular movement. One should be attentive to prevent the horse from crossing his hind legs behind each other or simply setting down his inside hind hoof near the outside. Tact is necessary. Forward movement should be kept.

In order to liberate a croup which resists, a demand of mobility of the jaw may be very instrumental (from horseback as well as on foot).

Side steps

The side steps of the Baucherist school are done almost 100% laterally, like in the side pass of Western riding (and as was the "croup to the wall" in La Guérinière's time). The horse should be kept as straight as possible.

This movement produces a spectacular elevation of the front end, because it bends the horse's hocks, and this is why: the hind joints of a horse are not built to bend laterally. Therefore, in this 100% lateral movement, the horse is obliged to rotate his croup in order to engage his crossing hind leg, but given the relative stiffness of the croup, the horse is also obliged to bend the stifle and hock of the other leg in order to allow the crossing hind leg to reach to the ground.

Counted walk

This expression is the translation of the French "pas compté." Some also say "pas écouté," but this latter expression is almost impossible to translate. "Ecouté" means "listened to," and "listened to walk" would not make any sense in English.

Why "listened to" (écouté)? Probably because horse and rider are kind of carefully listening to the slow cadence of the walk it is about. Perhaps, also, "écouté" is simply an alteration of "écourté," which means "shortened." This would make sense.

I prefer "pas compté," that is, "counted" walk, because when the exercise is well performed, each step of the horse should be "dropped," that is, allowed by the rider's hands carefully "filtrating" the forward movement, and therefore give the impression of a big, fat drop of liquid falling on the floor. The French for "eye dropper" is "compte-gouttes" ("drops counting device").

Like when using an eye dropper, the difficulty in the "counted walk" is twofold. If one presses too hard, the dripping gives way to a spurt (the horse falls onto his shoulders); if one does not squeeze enough, no drops come out (the horse stops).

The counted walk resembles the parade march of the British Grenadiers, hesitating, sliding from an instant of quasi-immobility to another instant of quasi-immobility.

The "counted walk" is the primary form of the "School walk."

I shall not elaborate more on this exercise, for fear of the misuse that can be made of it. I will only add this: it is very important *not to use the legs* during this exercise. Slowing the walk while pushing onto the bit would probably make the horse pace. On the contrary, when performed in the "release of the aids," the counted walk tends to diagonalize the gait. This can be used to teach a horse the "mobility in place," soft form of a piaffe.

From a counted walk it is very easy to engage a horse into a half-pass, even if he doesn't know the exercise, because the exquisite balance obtained by the counted walk lessens the difficulty any horse has to move laterally while bent in the direction of his march. This half-pass at a very slow walk is very likely to still increase the elevation of the withers you got from the previous counted walk on a straight line.

The "counted walk" was used by the Baucherist school's second "manner;" Beudant speaks of an "attentive, pompous, solemn march" (**Dressage du Cheval de Selle**, Berger-Levrault Publisher, 1948 edition, p. 58, translation is mine).

It was probably also practiced by the Old Masters. La Guérinière, to introduce the "shoulder-in," said that the horse will first be led along the wall "au petit pas lent et peu raccourci," which means, translated almost word for word, " slow walk, little shrunk."

This walk was probably some form of "counted walk."

The English translations of **Ecole de Cavalerie**, the one by Xenophon Press included, skirt the difficulty by translating the whole sentence as "collected walk".

There is probably no other way, but this translation offers the shortcoming of presenting collection, which for La Guérinière is an *end* for shoulder-in, as its *prerequisite*.

To give this chapter a conclusion, I would like to draw my readers' attention to the requirement, which we are constantly re-minded of, for a horse to keep his poll as the highest point of his neck curvature in order to display a correct attitude. This necessity has always been upheld by whichever school at whichever time, but I personally have never seen any author come up with even a hint of explanation for it. They just say it has to be so. Period. And no one objected, not even Baucher!

May I propose this explanation: isn't it because keeping the poll the highest point gives the rider a *guarantee* that the withers *won't drop?*

[1] As a matter of fact, a vertebral blocking situated as far as C1 ("atlas," next to the poll) may hamper the lifting of the wither's area.

[2] See **What the Horses Have Told Me** by Dr. Dominique Giniaux, English translation by J.-C. Racinet, 1996, Xenophon Press.

[3] Applying the spurs by a progressive pressure of their *neck* (and not by pricking) should not be impulsive, but on the contrary, keep the horse in place. Still, if the horse moves forward on this application of the spurs after obtaining the jaw flexion, *let him do it.*

[4] Lengthening the reins means *let them slide* between the fingers the necessary amount to make them *longer* (greater distance between the bit and the hand).

Chapter 9

Baucher and
the American Riding Tradition

Americans often complain that they have "no history" (as have, for instance, the European nations). It would be more accurate to say that they indeed have a history but don't care about it.

Let's consider Baucher, for instance. When Ivan Bezugloff asked me whether I would write a series of articles on Baucher, he read to me over the phone a letter from a *DRESSAGE & CT* reader who was intrigued with this name (Baucher) that he spotted here and there in dressage books, most of the time with some negative connotation.

Of course, I am very fortunate that this gentleman's curiosity gave me the opportunity to delve into the subject as I have done, but I must say that he could have found much by himself had he consulted the appropriate *American* documents.

But let's start with the beginning of my own quest for Baucher on this continent.

A few years ago, as I was giving a clinic in Pennsylvania, I was housed in a very quaint old country inn. There, I came across a magazine dated 1860 in which an article made express reference to Baucher as "the authority to consult when it comes to horses in Europe."

I already knew of the Baucherist influence in the US from a foreword by E. Schmit Jensen to **Breaking and Riding** (edition 1953) by James Fillis (the book was first published in 1902). Wrote Jensen: "Prior to starting the Cavalry School at Fort Riley at the beginning of this century an American Army Commission visited the various European Schools, including the Russian, to study their methods. It was Fillis' method that was adopted for Fort Riley with **Breaking and Riding** as the official text book."

Let us recall for the "lay rider" that James Fillis (1834-1913), an Englishman who lived mostly in France (where he showed at the circus), was a student of a student of Baucher and became the official Chief Instructor of the Russian Cavalry School in St. Petersburg from 1898 to 1910.

Yet with Fillis, the Baucherist influence in the United States remained indirect and, in my opinion as I shall explain later on, somewhat "warped."

A student and friend of mine once got the idea of looking in old dictionaries for the name Baucher, and not surprisingly, he found it.

"BAUCHER, François, a French teacher of horsemanship, born at Versailles about the beginning of this century, died in 1873. He invented a system of equine gymnastics, a portion of which, the method of suppling the horse's neck and jaw, has passed into general use and is adopted by every skillful trainer of riding horses. By a progressive series of flexions, the muscles are made so supple and yielding that the animal ceases to bear or pull upon the bit; while by the application of the whole system he comes to have no will except that of his rider. Baucher was repeatedly employed by the French Government to train horses for the cavalry service; but the refinements of his method were not suited to that purpose. He had many partisans in foreign countries, and was a personal favorite with the Duke of Wellington. He wrote in defence of his system, and his **Méthode d'équitation basée sur de nouveaux principes** (Paris, 1842; 11th ed. 1959) has been translated into many languages. In the United States it has been published under the title **Method of Horse-manship on New Principles** (Philadelphia, 1852)" (from the 1880 issue of **The American Encyclopedia,** D. Appleton and Company, New York).

But here comes a more important trove, which was discovered by another friend (and student) of mine in a local library, namely the official manual of the US Cavalry School at Fort Riley. Edited by Gordon Wright, it was published in 1962 by Simon and Schuster.

This book is deeply influenced by the French School of Horse-manship, which itself reflects much of the Baucherist philosophy.

Which amounts to saying that this **Manual for the American Cavalry** is more than tainted with Baucherism. And it is about the second "manner" to boot. Here are a few quotes:

Hand without legs, legs without hand

"The repeated countermanding" with the hand "of this increase in impulsion as soon as it is demanded" by the legs "soon results in the failure to obtain it in spite of the demands of the legs, whose effectiveness is soon decreased" (p. 56).

Fixed hand

"When the hand becomes active for any purpose, it is just moved the distance necessary to a position where it can best act to produce the result desired on the horse's movement. Then, assuming that the reins are properly stretched and adjusted in length, the half relaxed fingers close and tighten on them. Finally, the hand is 'fixed' in place, maintaining the additional resistance thus produced against the mouth with the bit. This increased resistance continues until the horse obeys the hand, whereupon the fingers immediately relax as a reward for obedience" (p. 763). One feels as if one is reading Faverot de Kerbrech himself!

Yielding of the jaw

"When the horse does not at once obey the action of the hand, it continues to 'resist' by remaining flexed. It steadily maintains the increased tension in the taut rein at exactly the same intensity until the horse yields. A series of pull and giving never teach a horse anything. Often with the fixed hand, the fingers may 'work the bit' a trifle to breakup tactfully the resistance of the horse's jaw, as will be discussed under 'vibrations.' The intensity of the hand's resistance must be just equal to that offered by the horse, never more" (p. 77).

"The ability to fix the hand in the necessary place, with a resistance exactly equal to the horse's resistance, and to yield the exact instant the horse yields, is the whole secret of an 'educated hand.' Without this ability, the true art of riding, and the feeling given by a perfect mouth, are unknown" (p. 77, italics are mine).

"To recapitulate, the keynote of educated hand is 'resistance,' not 'pulling.' To establish only the resistance equal to the force with which the horse is opposing the rider's, will require a 'fixed hand.' The 'fixed hand' is placed in the appropriate position to obtain a certain reaction from the horse" (p. 77).

[122]

Looking for the jaw flexion independently from the arching of the neck and as a prerequisite to it

"One of the greatest errors committed in using the 'fixed hand', is that of having the rein too short when the resistance is set up. Never ending effort should be made to avoid arching the horse's neck too much" (p. 79).

"It is surprising how quickly, with a little patience, a horse can be taught to yield to the bit with long reins, while keeping his neck extended" (p. 79).

"When the fingers are closed on the adjusted reins, a well trained horse, instead of resisting their action by contracting his jaw, relaxes it. His mouth partly opens and he gently closes his jaw again and softly chews once or twice on the bit as though feeling it, to be sure the rider has loosened the reins. *This softening or flexion of the jaw should always precede the arching, or 'direct flexion' of the neck at the poll*" (p. 80, italics are mine).

About these last three citations, it will be noticed that they abide by Baucher's concern for a strict separation of the flexion of the jaw from the direct flexion of the neck or even poll.

But whereas Baucher wanted to obtain this separation by an *upward* development of the neck, that is, its elevation, the editor or editors of these cavalry regulations did wisely opt for a *longitudinal* extension of the neck because of the possible dangers, for inexpert riders, of elevating the horse's head.

This concern is absolutely justified, although experience has shown the author that the yielding of the jaw is more difficult to obtain when the neck is low than when it is high, and more so with a mere snaffle.

Vibrations as a means of training, to be discarded when the horse is fully trained

This is Faverot de Kerbrech, 100 percent.

"As stated, after having perfected the lesson of relaxing the jaw in answer to vibrations, it will be found that soon the same result is obtained by simply increasing the tension in the reins. Vibrations are a means to an end, and with the trained horse, are only resorted to from time to time, when it is necessary to break up an occasional stubborn or whimsical stiffening of the jaw, to which any horse inevitably will return" (p. 82).

I hope I have persuaded my readers of the overall Baucherist second "manner" tone of these American Cavalry regulations. Let me now present the ultimate proof.

The document introduces a notion I had never heard of before, the "gather." I did not understand exactly what it meant until I read what follows, which showed me that "gather" was the American substitute for the French "ramener."

"The gather, as it is understood in higher equitation, is not concerned with the direction of the head alone. It concerns itself as much in the submission of the jaw, which is the first articulation (or spring) to receive the effect of the hand. If this spring responds with softness to the actions which solicit its play, it will bring about the flexibility of the neck and will provoke the tying to it of all the other parts, because of the relationship existing among all the muscles. If to the contrary, the jaw resists and refuses to be mobile, then there will be no more lightness, for by nature the resistances mutually

[124]

sustain themselves, and one resistance will set up numerous others. Thus in higher equitation, the 'gather' represents a general state of submission of all parts of the horse rather than a fixed direction of the head" (p. 87-88).

I happen to know very well General L'Hotte's **Questions Equestres** (Equestrian Questions), a posthumous book published in 1904 which is the Bible of many a French military rider, and I can assure the reader that this paragraph is the *exact translation* (with only one minor error I will not elaborate on) *of an excerpt of General L'Hotte's book.*

Wrote indeed General L'Hotte (I quote only the beginning and the end of the passage): "Le ramener, tel que le comprend la haute équitation, ne se concentre pas dans la direction de la tête. Il reside, tout d'abord dans la soumission de la mâchoire, qui est le premier ressort recevant l'effet de la main..."

"...Ainsi, en équitation savante, ce que le ramener représente, c'est bien moins une direction invariable de la tête qu'un etat général de soumission des ressorts."

So we are led to understand that Baucher always presided over the American Cavalry conception of High Equitation and horse training. He was somewhat present by the very beginning of Fort Riley, through the influence of Fillis, and was visibly still more (and in my opinion, in a much better way) present by the end of the existence of this school, as shown by the document I have quoted, which is nothing but an adaptation, to military purposes, of the Baucherism second "manner."

My readers have probably understood that I have some misgivings about James Fillis. Please let me elaborate on them for a short while.

[125]

Born in England in 1834, Fillis had come to France at a rather early age, since, after having first worked at the circus under the (prestigious) tutelage of Laurent Franconi—the very same Franconi who had introduced the young Baucher to the Circus—he was around 1855 (the date of Baucher's famous accident) taking lessons from François Caron, one of Baucher's first pupils.

After Baucher's retirement and death, Fillis himself became a very famous circus rider, acquiring a great reputation in France and other European countries, Germany in particular.

Although performing on the circular (and small, 15 yards in diameter) arena of the circus, Fillis would mostly train his horses outside (probably a matter of genes—he was an Englishman, wasn't he?). Although using the flexions of Baucher, but on a beforehand reasonably elevated neck, his trainings differ from Baucher's by the fact that they were using the movement from the very beginning.

"Finally, the work of making the horse go forward constitutes the great difference between my system of equitation and that of Baucher.

"My first lesson has been to make the animal go forward...

"We shall subsequently see that this difference in method is found in all the work" (**Breaking and Riding**, pp. 63 and 64).

This difference is so important that it—in my opinion—excludes Fillis from the Baucherist school *stricto sensu*. For Baucher, the movement is a result, not a means. Baucher did use many different procedures; their set constantly evolved. Some were added, some were modified, and some were discarded, but he never wavered on the philosophy, which was to establish balance prior to asking for movement.

Since Baucher was a seeker, this very notion of balance also evolved and refined itself progressively. In the beginning, this balance was, in his mind, only a balance of *weight:* the four limbs of the horse had to be equally loaded, which was to be obtained by the "effet d'ensemble." Then the balance became more a balance of *forces*, the lightness of the jaw allowing the rider to "absorb" with his hands the thrust of the hind legs. Finally, the notion of balance took on a *physiological* dimension; the horse would find his balance when he was *relaxed* or, to use the more precise French expression, "décontracté" (de-contracted).

The notion of relaxation led to a refinement in the flexion of the jaw, whose "mobility" was more looked for than its opening, leading with the fully trained horse to a "light murmur" (General L'Hotte) or even a "smile" (Beudant).

It also led to the "release of the aids," mostly the legs, the horse then performing "as if on his own will." It led to "hand without legs, legs without hand." It finally led to the "separation of force from movement," acted out by frequent periods of immobility during which the horse would rest not only his body but *also his mind*.

All this is foreign to Fillis. From Baucher, he keeps only the proceedings, those of the first "manner," and the most questionable ones, like the "strong attacks" with the spurs, or the jaw flexion as an opening (a gaping?) rather than a relaxation.

To make myself better (and definitely, I hope) understood on what the gist of Baucher's philosophy is, I will use a comparison drawn from military history. Everybody knows how disciplined the German Army has always been. Up to the end of World War II, its discipline was pretty much following the Prussian tradition; it was forceful, unforgiving, and based on punishment. Then after the war, to change this image, the German Army adopted a new system, which it called the "innere Führung" ("inner lead"). In this system, the constraints of discipline should not be felt any longer as coming from outside but from inside the subject submitting to it.

The same type of difference separates Baucher's system from all the other systems: while they try to fashion the horse via outside constraints, he tries to work the horse "from inside" ("position precedes action").

So Baucher is not the enemy of movement; he is simply the enemy of any movement performed in dubious or unsatisfactory conditions. In other words, he never compromises on balance.

Fillis' system differs from Baucher's on this crucial issue and therefore, in my opinion, *cannot* be called Baucherist anymore, in spite of all the similarities. Fillis works "from outside," and often forcefully.

Fillis would make permanent use of his legs, whose power he doesn't seem to have ever questioned. On "school walk," for instance, he writes: "To obtain the school walk we should use the legs energetically and the hands moderately; should make numerous movements with the horse's whole body by means of this aid." And in a footnote, he adds: "By this I mean the movement of the horse as a whole which brings him into hand, namely, to send him by the legs on the hand and to send a part of the impulsion from the hands to our legs" (op. cit., p. 118).

For those who have seen the majesty and grace of a school walk ridden in a total release of the aids, by some equerries of the "Cadre Noir" or by Maestro Nuno Oliveira, these lines have an almost blasphemous tone!

One wonders how this permanent use of the legs did not have for Fillis the "blunting" effect it has for any other rider. The explanation is simple: Fillis (whose equestrian tact is not to be questioned) would train only Thoroughbreds, and crazy ones at that, as he would boast. This option obligatorily diminishes the value of his message, since a school leader should offer a method useful to the lay rider on the ordinary horse.

Certainly, Fillis obtained great results from his horses, namely all the artificial movements which Baucher had brought into fashion, like cantering rearward or on three legs, etc. But I hold that *any* very talented rider on carefully selected subjects can teach *anything* to a horse. It is only a question of will. The method, then, matters very little. At the time Fillis was Equerry of the Tsar in St. Petersburg, there was in Saumur a young captain by the name of Jacques de Saint Phalle, who had been challenged by Fillis himself to realize, after one year of training, the following stunt: canter on three legs, canter backwards, flying changes cantering backwards. On August 17, 1905, he won the challenge. Rumor has it that the fatigue brought about by this endeavor started the deterioration of his health which was to bring him to his grave three years later.

Now, de Saint Phalle was not a Baucherist, and never became a school founder, although he had written a book on the *"training and use of the riding horse"* (1899).

There is nowadays in France a gentleman by the name of Mario Luraschi who trains horses for the cinema: he teaches them how to rear, fall, sit, lie down, etc. Since he is extremely talented, he also practices some of the stunts "à la Baucher": Spanish walk backwards, reversed pirouettes on three legs, etc.

Now, Mario Luraschi admits that he opened his first dressage book 20 years after he had started training horses in this way, and adds that he was rather befuddled by its reading!

But he specifies that he works only Andalusian horses, which he himself carefully selects in Spain directly.

I mention this to bolster my statement that a lot of talent plus a lot of determination plus a carefully selected horse can make up for the absence of principles; Mr. Luraschi is perhaps the reincarnation of Jacques de Saint Phalle but, like him, probably won't found a school. Back to Fillis.

It seems to me that Fillis was an unquiet rider, a "doer," who would "make" the horse do and not "let" the horse do. The whole atmosphere of the second "manner," whose axiom was "placer et laisser faire" ("position the horse and let him do"), therefore remained a mystery for him.

He stated that "It is simply absurd to say that the complete 'rassembler' can be obtained by the hands without the legs, or by the

Fig. 22 - James Fillis performing a piaffe; right diagonal in the air.

Fig. 23 - Capt. Beudant on Mabrouck, performing an excellent piaffe.

legs without the hands" (op. cit., p. 340). Yet by carefully abiding by this principle, Captain Marcel Beudant, no later than ten or fifteen years later, would make him a liar and perform with all his horses exactly the same acrobatic movements which Fillis was so proud of.

But the style was much different. Even in the most difficult movements, Beudant always looked as if he were resting on horse-back. To illustrate my talk I produce here two copies of photographs of piaffe performed by each of those great equerries.

As a conclusion for this chapter, I would like to evoke a person-ality of the riding community of Michigan, namely Major Borg. I met him once when I was residing in that state some eight years ago.

Major Borg had an accident with an obstinate horse and can no longer walk, let alone ride. He had been one of the foremost riders in the United States Army, having placed fourth with *Klingsor* in the 1948 London Olympics for the last Army Olympic team as a Lieutenant and 11th with *Bill Biddle* in the 1952 Helsinki Olympics as a civilian competitor.

Now, in spite of his infirmity, Major Borg still trains horses, and here is how. Next to the entrance of the indoor arena, he stands in a booth in such a position that his hands are level with the mouth of the horse he is working. The booth pivots around a central vertical axis.

So Major Borg flexes his horse's jaw and poll, and when movement is necessary, he makes the booth turn around itself, in a combination of Pluvinel (work around one pillar), and Baucher or Fillis (flexions).

Then after a while, Major Borg calls an aide, who rides the horse under his control. If some aspect of this work is not satisfactory, the aide dismounts, and Major Borg flexes the horse anew. And so on.

When I saw this, I understood immediately that the message of Baucher had certainly been carried to this continent. Long since!

Chapter 10

Practical Baucherism

My primary goal, when I am lucky enough to give a series of "clinics" at the same riding school, is to improve my students' riding style, since awkwardness and rudeness of the rider's hand is the most common cause of a horse's imbalance.

A good horsemanship, that is, *a riding of lightness*, should abide by the principles of release, separation, and moderation of the aids and be served by a good position.

The first of these principles requires the systematic disengagement of the aids as soon as they have been obeyed. The aids should start, restore, and transform; they should never *maintain* any given situation. The horse should not be carried by the rider's hands and legs; he should constantly be left free to perform *on his own* what he has been required to by the aids.

The second principle holds that hands and legs should be used separately as often as possible, namely that no impulsive demand with the legs should *ever* bump into the refusal of the hands.

By requiring moderation in the wielding of the aids, the third principle simply expresses that the aids work out of "quality" and not "quantity."

Finally, a good position is necessary. It proceeds from pliability on horseback added to the correct position of the torso, the forwarding of the hips, and the almost total relaxation of the rider's thighs and calves.

If constantly ridden in this way, horses acquire balance, self-impulsion, and a beginning of self-carriage; last but not least, they retrieve their "joie de vivre."

Of course, there are exceptions. *Georgio* was one of them. Imagine a Frisian crossed with a Belgian and then crossed again with a Mustang; the result will probably look like *Georgio*. *Georgio* is small and solid black; he has feathers on his fetlocks, a bony croup, steep shoulders, a short neck, and a large, flat forehead. A very intelligent little cookie, he figured out ages ago that the best way to save his physical integrity, at least as concerns his teeth, lies in clenching his jaws, stiffening his poll, and pulling straight forward as much as he can, so much so that he happened several times to literally fall down to the ground on the straight at a trot, entangled in his own hooves.

One day, a student of mine by the name of Mary-Helen, decided to buy *Georgio*. Love is blind.

In order to help her give *Georgio* some balance, I showed her how to flex the horse's lower jaw, at a halt, on foot, and then on horseback with a simple snaffle. I told her to do it systematically before riding and then, when riding, to ask for a yielding of the jaw before any movement she would perform. I explained to her that it was very important not to "pull" and to work hard because it would take some time before she could master the technique. And off I went.

When I came back one month later, I was amazed at *Georgio*'s transformation. He was really looking great; his balance was incredibly better. I asked Mary-Helen to show me how she was asking for the yielding of the jaw. It was good, but not perfect; she was still pulling a little. Yet only an approximate flexion of the jaw had led to this spectacular result.

After one more month of the same proceedings, Mary-Helen would participate in her first dressage show, and place second to boot! And now, lo and behold, *Georgio* also *jumps*!

If all the hardships, bitter fights against jealousy and sometimes calumny, and hard work of Baucher had resulted only in this, it would already have been worthwhile.

And now, another story in the same vein. It features *Sweet William,* an elegant, 16.2 chestnut horse with Quarterhorse, Thoroughbred, and Arabian blood in the veins, if memory serves. When he was brought to me, *William* had developed bad habits and had become almost impossible to ride outside on the trail, where he would swerve and buck for no (human) reason. His owners were almost desperate, since they did not want to part with the horse, whom they loved.

The first time I rode the horse, the vast indoor arena of the New Jersey riding facility where I was teaching at the time emptied out in less than five minutes. The horse was all over the place—in one word: dangerous.

William's owners would not say a word; huddled in a corner, they were gaping in puzzlement. They had probably thought I would ride the horse "energetically," force him into his gaits, put up a big fight, and drive the rascal into submission by the sheer strength of my seat, legs, and biceps. I didn't. I worked by "bits and buts," an expression twice descriptive of this technique: flexing the jaw at a halt ("bits") and then pushing for a slow walk or trot ("buts"). I would move the horse on side steps, then ask for a departure in a canter, and then stop the canter immediately. I would ask again for relaxation, etc. Above all, I would never accept making more than one stride with a *contracted* horse.

Speaking of the owners, I remember telling my wife, "they won't come again." I was wrong. Exactly one week later, a Saturday, they were there again with *William:* "Please, work him."

I did. And the like every Saturday. I explained to *William's* owners that from a technical point of view as well as for the sake of their own wallet, they would be better off entrusting me with *William's* training for a few months, but in vain. They wanted to enjoy *William*, inasmuch as the news was encouraging: *William* would swerve less often and less dangerously; he had quit bolting away. By my 13th Saturday, *William* gave me his first strides of passage and his first canter flying changes of lead. Then I had to leave New Jersey and move to South Carolina, where I own a house. This spaced out my working sessions with *William*, which could only occur when I would go back to New Jersey for a clinic. So all in all, in two years, I have added perhaps 15-20 other hours of work on *William*, and I happen to have passed flying changes every other stride with him. This does not mean that I am such a good rider; this means that *William* is a good horse, and that Baucher's second "manner" really works. It has so far worked as well for the owners, who can ride the horse as much as they please, and this is my best reward.

But there is more: one day, as I was about to work *William* in a clinic, I was warned that big blue barrels had been set up on the arena and that he was dead scared of them. "He won't come closer than 50 feet to them."

I was pretty sure that I could solve the problem rapidly, and at first I tried by the usual ways, using my seat, legs, and voice and trying to "channel" the horse between my reins, but in vain: the horse was *really* afraid and was showing me that he meant business.

Suddenly, I realized that under the circumstances, I was not faithful to my own philosophy, so I asked *William* for a yielding of the jaw and pushed him forward in the direction of the object of his fear. After a yielding of the jaw, a horse *cannot* resist the action of the rider's legs. So it worked for a few steps, whereupon *William* froze again. I reiterated my demand for yielding, then went a few more steps, up to a new "freezing," etc...and in this calm way, without using force, I brought *William*'s nose practically over the barrel.

This reinforced in me the belief that a horse light on the bit is much more under the influence of his rider than a horse who takes a strong contact.

A third example: years ago, when I was in Michigan, one of my students was having problems with her horse, a very low-spirited "mustang" mare. As in the case of *Georgio*, observance of the principles of release, separation, and moderation of the aids had worked only up to a point. The fact was that the mare had very poor balance, and this was not likely to improve her impulsion.

Now, I have omitted telling you that my student was very keen on showing, every Saturday and Sunday if possible, even though at a low level. This eagerness to show helped me persuade her to employ in her training any means, even unconventional, which could better her mare's balance.

I thus persuaded her to resort to the lifting of her mare's neck and head, at a halt, according to Baucher's second "manner." The results came as expected; she scored better and better, so much so that in the end she wound up champion for the year of the regional dressage association for her level.

I laughed, imagining the face that the judges who were acknowledging these progresses would have made, had they known by which means they had been obtained.

Baucherism—that is, in essence, the mobility of the jaw as a prerequisite to any exercise—may also be of great help for higher level movements. With the lightness of mouth, piaffe and passage can be taught to good horses in a very short time—sometimes in one working session only. And this without the help of a man on foot, and the rider having only *one* dressage whip in hand, if any.

These results could make one believe in the advantage of Baucherism in the training of a horse with the purpose of showing "dressage." But this is probably too optimistic a statement, and I would limit my conclusion by saying that they are demonstrative of the progresses in impulsion, balance, and brilliance that may be obtained by Baucherist procedures; how these progresses would be acknowledged by the judges is another story that I would like to examine here more thoroughly.

First this: if those of my students who were performing dressage before they knew me most of the time see their performances improving on the competition grounds, the good marks they earn are invariably accompanied by the following "restrictive" comment: "Should make more use of his/her legs!"

This, in my opinion, only reflects the ignorance of the judges. Of course, they know their job. But they know only one style that they have a mission to enforce. They ignore that a horse can perfectly be and remain "on the bit" *without being constantly pushed onto this bit by the rider's legs;* they ignore that the best way to make a horse lose his impulsion is, as it happens, to try to *maintain* this impulsion by a constant application of the legs.

They abide by the modern German philosophy of dressage, but they ignore that it was precisely a German, Baron de Sind, who, way before Baucher, wrote this: "A perfectly trained horse doesn't need anymore the aid of the legs; and any objection one may desire to oppose me with this regard will always be belied by my horses, who certainly do not go by rote." (**L'Art du Manège**, 1774. The author was German, but the book was written in French. English translation is mine.)

This leads me to think that, at a higher level, between two movements performed with an equal brilliance by two horses, of whom one would be ridden with evident and constant application of the aids and the other ridden in "liberty on parole" (that is, in the "release of the aids"), the judges would unfortunately prefer the former over the latter.

True, the official texts request that the aids be unobtrusive, but the very notion that the aids should be *absent* as long as there is no need for a *transition*, that is, a *modification* in the speed, gait, or movement, is foreign—nay, shocking—to the judges with the FEI label.

The notion of "release of the aids" ("descente des aides") is not well-received nowadays in dressage, release of the legs as I just mentioned, but also *and still more* release of the hand ("descente de main"). For instance, the FEI states that a piaffe should be performed with taut reins. So Maestro Oliveira, for instance, would have gotten bad marks for some of his (magnificent) piaffes, had he chosen to show.

This view—FEI's—is faithful to the teachings of the German Master Steinbrecht, who states that even between the pillars, a horse should be pushed constantly onto the ropes: "As under the rider, the only work between the pillars that is of true value for dressage is the work that the horse performs with a correct contact, here with the halter, a principle that one cannot call to mind often enough" (**The**

Gymnasium of the Horse, translated by Helen K. Gibble, Xenophon Press, 1995, p. 291).

Why is his view so prevalent? Why should only one style be acknowledged on the dressage rectangles? I don't know, and I must say that it has not always been so. In a previous chapter, I evoked the ambiance of equestrian friendship which existed in the 1930s between the representatives of the two main styles (there can be others) of riding.

This openmindedness shows very much in the good rankings obtained in *five* Olympic Games by Captain (1932,1936) and then Colonel (1948, 1952, 1956) André Jousseaume, who was fifth in 1932, fifth in 1936, second in 1948, third in 1952, and fifth in 1956. Although extremely talented, Jousseaume was perhaps not the most brilliant representative of the French style, but he was certainly the most consistent. Now, photographs we have of him as he performed show a horse almost artificially light, ridden with almost shockingly looped reins. For those who believe that Baucherism sets a horse behind the bit, let it be reminded that Andre Jousseaume was a great sports rider: an outstanding show jumping rider, he also won the French National Championship of "military" (three-day event) several times.

It is difficult to say when and why things turned out differently. The replacement of military riders with civilians in international competition after WWII was most detrimental to French dressage. Although a new trend seems to be appearing now, dressage has never been very popular with the French riding community. There was a big breach after Colonel Jousseaume's death (1960). Although it had kept a few horses until 1962, the French army was no longer the "mould" out of which dressage riders would be formed. Besides, post-colonial wars had kept its officers very busy; they had other fish to fry.

Surprisingly, the horsemanship of the French tradition, that is, in the words of Colonel (now retired General) Pierre Durand, then head of the Cadre Noir, "a moderate Baucherism grafted onto a classical trunk," found a refuge in Portugal.

A neutral power, Portugal escaped the hardships of WWII. Her army, though, due to the dictatorial nature of the government, remained very prominent in the nation until 1974 (the year a revolution took place in Lisbon). In addition, the riding tradition there has always been very lively, due probably to the popularity of bullfights, done only from horseback (whereas it is also, and much more, practiced on foot in Spain).

Portugal breeds the Lusitano, a cousin to the Andalusian horse. Everybody knows the role played by this type of horse in the dawning and developing of the art of classical equitation, from the 16th century on.

Dressage is very popular in Portugal, but its goal remains close to its origins: a horse is trained there to become a fighter. Now to describe the drift undergone by the notion of dressage, I ask the question: if you had to fight a bull, would you take a Hanoverian and push him constantly onto his bit in order to keep the reins taut?

Back to Baucher. Portuguese are pragmatic. Although they had the horse and the techniques developed in the baroque era to ride this horse, they manifested very early a vivid interest in Baucher and his techniques. And so Portugal realized the same "fusion" between the teachings of the classical era and the teachings of Baucher which, as quoted from Colonel Pierre Durand, ended up in a "moderate Baucherism grafted onto a classical trunk."

[141]

Still, this very brilliant horsemanship is ill-received in dressage competitions and is therefore obliged to express itself behind closed doors at home, fortunate if people come from abroad to see it.

Speaking of Portuguese Cavalry officers who compete on an international level, Diogo de Bragança writes: "Their tendency is to abide by the conceptions of the French School. If we see them adopt some procedures of the German School, it is because they are aware of the propensity of the judges to establish their rankings according to this latter's criteria" (**L'Equitation de Tradition Française,** 1975, p. 138, translation is mine).

Now that Nuno Oliveira has passed away, everybody, even in the official circles of the FEI, tends to refer to him as one of the glories of the classical art of dressage. This he certainly was. But no one wonders why this so talented and dedicated man *never showed on the FEI circuit*. Part of it came from his own reluctance, but another good part came from the ostracism he was submitted to. I read somewhere that for one of his later clinics in England (perhaps his last one), *not one member of the British Horse Society had deigned to attend*. As a well-intended German gentleman once wrote in *DRESSAGE & CT*: "Vive la difference!"

Should it be this way? I don't believe so. On page 151 of Sylvia Loch's book **Dressage, the Art of Classical Riding** (Trafalgar Square Publishing), there is a photograph of Otto Lörke riding at an extended trot with his reins completely looped, enough to make Colonel Jousseaume himself jealous!

Now if somebody can be called the father of modern German dressage, it is certainly Otto Lörke. He trained the two horses that won the Gold and the Silver in the Berlin Olympics (1936). He was the trainer of the German Olympic dressage team for 1936 (Gold),

1952 (Bronze), and 1956 (Silver). He was the teacher of the late Willy Schultheiss, who became the trainer of the German dressage team as of 1974.

By the end of the 1970s or the beginning of the '80s, I don't remember exactly, Willy Schultheiss came to Fontainebleau for a working session with the French dressage team. Although this session took place in private, I know from a participant that Schultheiss multiplied the "descentes de main" ("release of hand") in a very expert manner in order to show that when he had given a horse the proper balance, this balance was established for good.

In 1984, on the occasion of the Olympic Games in Los Angeles, Reiner Klimke was filmed as he was working a younger horse just for the sake of the matter and also as he was performing with *Ahlerich*. The first part was just delightful. His style was supple, light, very close indeed to that of Nuno Oliveira. Then came *Ahlerich*, the official test and the second part of the tape: you would have thought it was about another rider. This "other" rider won the Gold. That's what it was all about.

Now a last story: I cannot guarantee its authenticity, although I know it is true. Listen to this: the same prestigious German rider I just mentioned and the French Master Michel Henriquet (who was considered the foremost representative of Oliveira in France) were once having one of those heated discussions which only riders can have. As Henriquet wanted by all means to have his point of view prevail, his Olympic interlocutor simply said, "You are probably right. But my problem is this one: next Saturday, I have to show."

A last piece of information: the "descente de main" ("release of the hand") was, if not invented, at least first described by the French Master La Guérinière (1696-1751), *whom the Germans acknow-*

ledge.

So let me ask a question of my own in turn: is "descente de main" only for the photographs?

Chapter 11

Baucherism
and Competitive Dressage

T hus we have established that riding "in the release of aids" is not likely to be acknowledged by the dressage judges.

Now a still more serious problem lies in the progression of the training, as in the use of specific bittings. These two aspects are linked. In fact, they are so intermingled, that I will deal with both together.

Let us recall here that for a Baucherist, lightness is the name of the game, and that this notion does not limit itself to the fact that a horse is light *on his feet*, but that also, and as a condition for it, he is light *to the rider's hands*.

For the other school of thought, in the better case, lightness (as here above understood), appears by the end of the training. It is accepted that lightness does not have to be present in the first stages of the training, hence the progression from a thick, hollow-mouthed snaffle to a full bridle.

Three movements of "High School" characterize the high level tests of the FEI: canter pirouette, piaffe, and passage. They require a horse more seated on the haunches, and with them comes the full bridle. The rider has to be more efficiently equipped to better balance a horse heretofore not accustomed to working in this equilibrium.

This, as I explained in Chapter 8, requires a horse constantly "on the bit," that is, constantly "collectable" by means of half-halts.

To the notion of an "on the bit" horse, the Baucherists prefer the notion of "in hand," which means that the horse's balance is constantly checked by means of mobilization of the lower jaw. And since the yielding of the jaw is more easily realized, at first, with a double bridle, this set of bits appears much earlier in the Baucherist progression.

This is not to say that lightness, understood as the constant possibility for the rider to mobilize his horse's lower jaw, cannot be obtained with a simple snaffle, but it takes more time and patience; it is less immediate, so much so that it seems more logical, for a Baucherist, to start the training with a double bridle (that is to say, as soon as the horse's mouth can accept it), and to perfect it, much later on, with a simple snaffle. Although this opinion may surprise many nowadays, it is not devoid of pertinence. Is it not a proof of technical achievement when the same result, or more, is obtained with lesser means (snaffle vs. double bridle)?

For instance, do we imagine a sculptor starting a statue with a fine chisel and finishing it with a strong one? Of course not. And why should it be different as we fashion a horse?

Writes Beudant: "The snaffle is softer, it pains less than the curb, only when used as a halter merely to guide the horse. When it is substituted for the curb, it is severer than the latter. I grant that in expert hands, the snaffle readily destroys all resistances, but generally, the mouth made with the curb is ready for the snaffle, while a lower jaw that gives to the snaffle often resists the curb unless specially prepared for it. The reason for the soft mouths of horses ridden by Arabs is that their horses are always ridden with the curb bit. It is the exception when one sees an Arab's horse boring on the bit. In training, it is more practicable to begin with the curb and later to change to the snaffle" (**Horse Training, Outdoor and High-School**, translation by Lt. Col. John A. Barry, US Cavalry, pp. 43-44).

Horse Training, Outdoor and High-School was published in 1923. In 1929, Beudant wrote a very short and condensed manual titled **Dressage du Cheval de Selle (Training of the Saddle Horse)**, in which he wrote: "In the schooling, the flexions of the jaw come about more easily with the curb than with the snaffle. However, Baucher was not mistaken when he told the future General L'Hotte: 'The bridoon, it is so good!' Indeed, in the seeking for *ramener*, the hand must act alone without the help of the rider's legs and it should not allow the horse's head to come nearer the vertical line before the lightness being perfect. Now, the surest means for this result is the use of the snaffle, the simple bridoon, by the hand fixed very high which gives the maximum of elevation of the neck as well as lightness; then only one lets the head take its most becoming position, vertical or thereabout" (translation is mine).

Written only six years after the first quotation, this latter excerpt seems at first glance somewhat contradictory to the former, yet the contradiction is smaller than it appears. Here, Beudant deals with the seeking of *ramener at a halt*, or at a very slow walk or trot, as a consequence of the flexion of the lower jaw in a very high position of head, whereupon the rider lowers the hand, lengthens somewhat the reins, and leaves the horse alone *as long as the lightness remains unaltered*.

This, of course, can be perfectly done with a simple snaffle. Another thing is, however, to keep the lightness unaltered with a simple snaffle when the action is somewhat increased. In this case, the double bridle retrieves all its value.

Let me here quote Sylvia Loch: "The double bridle, or gentlemen's bridle, became the brunt of a new prejudice (this has continued to the present day). Some regarded its use almost as a form of cheating; and regardless of a horse's conformation, age or mouth, and the use to which it might be put, you were all at once no good as a rider unless you used the snaffle. Thus the bit designed for the racetrack or steeplechase became the everyday bit of the twentieth century.

"This led to complacency. In the old days, riders of every nationality had respected the use of the curb. Hunting and manège riders alike prided themselves on their ability to handle the reins with finesse. 'He has good hands' was the accolade every horseman aspired to, and the constant exhortation to lighter hands not only echoed from the walls of the riding school, but was passed on from father to son, mother to daughter, in every riding family. *With the coming of the snaffle, most of this natural respect for the horse's mouth disappeared completely*." (**Dressage**, Trafalgar Square Publishing, 1990, p. 130, italics are mine.)

The transition "collected trot-extended trot-collected trot" on the diagonal comes in the Third Level, Test 1, which must be ridden with a simple snaffle. From a Baucherist point of view, lightness, i.e., *the mobility of the jaw*, should never be lost during this transition (that is, that no half-halt should be required to return to collection after the extension).

Beudant would probably have been capable of doing this with a plain snaffle. But let us acknowledge that a horse who, mouthed with a simple snaffle, can pass from collection to extension and again to collection on a short distance, *without losing its lightness*, i.e., ridden throughout this transition on *the mere weight of the reins*, would have attained what Baucher called the "equilibrium of the first genre," and therefore would be *ipso facto ready for the Grand Prix* and more, and moreover would not need for this to be ridden at any further time in a double bridle.

To sum myself up on this important point of the "mouthing," I hold that:

1) The snaffle is mandatory up to Third Level *because lightness is not a part of the program.*

2) If lightness were part of the program, the double bridle should be authorized much earlier in the progression.

3) If lightness (horse ridden on the "weight of the reins," no half-halts necessary *ever),*and the mere use of the snaffle were together required, *then the progression would lose all purpose,* and the horse would be immediately ready for high performances. (In contrast, we would have to wait some time before showing.)

What prevents, as it happens, a horse from performing such and such a movement of the Grand Prix, for instance, is not the fact that he has not been taught this movement but the fact that *he still doesn't have the balance required by the said movement.* The purpose of the progression is to make him acquire the balance little by little. Therefore each movement of the progression is (ever so slightly) *forced upon the horse.*

The only thing which is forced upon a horse in the Baucherist method is the lightness of the jaw, which should never quit. This, of course, also entails a progression in the movements, but

1) it cannot be the same (for instance, extended gaits should only be performed by the end of the training) and

2) the use of the double bridle should be authorized to facilitate

the process.

In his book **Dressage** (which has been translated into English), Colonel Jousseaume, whose riding was very influenced by Baucherism, proposes a progression noticeably different from that of the FEI. It comprises six "periods." The extended trot intervenes only by the fourth period. The canter pirouettes intervene only by the sixth period, together with…the canter in place and the canter backwards!

I have reported in a previous chapter that Col. Jousseaume participated in five Olympic Games, with three fifths, one third, and one second place. He was lucky that he could engage directly in the Grand Prix. Nowadays, he probably could not show, due to the difference between his progression of training and that imposed by the official texts.

A last observation: in his book **My Horses, My Teachers**, Col. Alois Podhajsky shows a photograph of his horse *Nero*, with whom he won the Bronze in Berlin (1936) after one year of training; in the photo, the horse was already ridden in double bridle.

And perhaps it is this very fact that allowed the horse to make rapid progress and earn the Bronze medal.

So we are in the presence of two men, at least, from two different schools, let's bear in mind, who nowadays, in spite of their capability, which was acknowledged by their outstanding records, *could not show at the FEI level*, let alone the Olympic Games. They were lucky enough that they were from the "aristocracy" of their sport, both of them belonging to prestigious Riding Academies (Saumur and Vienna).

But now, the only way to rise to prominence is to go on the show circuit and win. They, in this case, would have had to change their training system, more so, of course, for Colonel Jousseaume.

This observation makes us measure the extent of the dictator-ship which is imposed upon dressage by the acknowledgement of one and only one progression, one and only one style. Those who accept this style and progression feel, of course, at home on the dressage rectangle. The others are unfortunately *pushed into marginalization*, not because they lack knowledge or riding ability but because their style will not be taken into consideration.

This mass of "marginalized" riders is growing every day. I meet many of them on the occasion of my clinics all around the US. Their story is remarkably stereotyped. They have started by showing, year after year. But since they do not have the real "dressage horse," nor the finances to buy such a horse, they feel condemned to First Level Test One forever, because try as they may to push their gangly TB onto the thick snaffle/drop noseband with their legs, *no progress comes about.*

And so they drop out, change the bit, or ride for pleasure, and all of a sudden, they witness a breakthrough: they get their first flying change, or they teach their horses how to passage, or whatever.

This fills them with joy, but they can't help feeling somewhat melancholy thinking that no judge will ever sanction their endeavor or give them the "pat on the shoulder" they so richly deserve.

Is there hope for these "outcasts," whom I would like to group under the heading of "Oliveirists," even if they have never taken any lesson from the late Portuguese Master, even if they ignore his very name, because he certainly was the figurehead of this renascent "Roman School?" Yes, there is hope, if the FEI and the dressage establishment at large accept their style, accept *two progressions*, that which is already enforced and another one studied for them and their horses. The two progressions would lead to the Grand Prix as

[151]

we know it, and I am sure that the competition would be most enhanced by this friendly rivalry.

May I one more time quote Sylvia Loch? "If some positive changes could be made within these suggested guidelines, the two schools of thought would blend to the satisfaction of all. *As long, however, as we remain complacent to the present system of training, judging and the presentation and scoring of tests, there must inevitably follow a polarization of the two systems*" (op. cit., p. 213, italics are mine).

As we near the end of this study on Baucher and his methods, there remain two questions to be addressed: does Baucherism reduce drastically the length of training, and does it allow one to train *all* horses, even the least talented?

In answer to these questions, I can only give a personal opinion, and here is why: Baucherism is *dead*. By this I mean that it is very unlikely that there might remain, somewhere in the world, a rider who can claim a *direct filiation* to Baucher, a student of a student...of a student of Baucher himself.

I happen to have known one of them. His name was Jean Landrin. He was a well-to-do farmer of northern France. Rather advanced in age when I made his acquaintance, he would not ride any longer but would still train horses on foot, an exercise in which he was very skilled. He contacted me because I had a horse that looked exactly like one of his, and he wanted to work them in "tandem." I sold him the horse.

He used to tell me that he had believed he knew how to ride until he was 50; then he met Colonel de T., who initiated him to Baucherism, the first "manner." "Then I understood," he would add, "that I had heretofore really known nothing about riding." He would tell me, "I am of the fourth generation in direct filiation after Baucher." Baucher had formed Raabe, who had formed Colonel X., who had formed Colonel de T. I was always very moved when he would tell me that.

He was very eager to have me ride one of his horses. On my side, I was very apprehensive, but I could not let him down, so I agreed to try. He provided me with dreadful five spike rowel spurs. I was almost terrified, and I did as little as I could, short of offending him.

Jean Landrin passed away a few months later, so I lost forever the opportunity I could have taken advantage of: exchanging ideas and information with a man who had received the Baucherist message in direct transmission.

Now back to our subject.

General Decarpentry is one of the best sources of information we have on Baucher, because his grandfather, Eugene Caron, was one of the first students of the illustrious Master. Caron took careful notes, which Decarpentry had access to. So we learn that Baucher would sell to Caron—and others—the horses whose training he didn't want to pursue due to their lack of physical ability, which prevented them from being presented in public, or because of some heretofore concealed defect.

Wrote Caron, "Baucher does not like to sell in Paris the horses he gets rid of, and prefers to see them go as far away as possible, deep in some Province" (op. cit., p. 153, translation is mine).

One can certainly understand that due to the exigencies of his career, Baucher couldn't afford to spend time on horses whose training was, at first, disappointing. More than likely, had he persevered on them, his powerful means of training would have produced the expected result, but *it would have taken time.*

[153]

Still, Baucher is famous for having trained in a very short time some horses endowed with very bad reputations: *Gericault*, whose training took one month before he could be shown at the circus; *Kleber*, a stallion whose gaits were "lost" and whose training, undertaken upon a bet, also lasted one month before he could be presented successfully at the circus; and, of course, the outstanding *Partisan*, perhaps Baucher's best horse. A Thoroughbred imported from England for a hefty sum of money, *Partisan* had successively disappointed all of his owners and riders because of his fighting and rearing, and he was finally sold to Baucher for a cheap price.

You must excuse my playing the devil's advocate, but two questions arise. First, what were the nature and quality of these accelerated trainings? Second, how bad were those horses really before being trained by Baucher?

Partisan's training was very sophisticated, very "scientific," and it comprised a number of new and revolutionary airs. But could *Partisan* have been ridden easily, even for ordinary riding, by anybody else than Baucher? This is not sure. Let me remind you how puzzled the most prominent equerry of Saumur's "Cadre Noir," Commandant (Major) Rousselet, was upon riding Baucher's other famous horse *Capitaine*.

Kleber's training was probably less sophisticated than that of *Partisan*, but perhaps more artificial, that is, more focused on what is necessary to a horse performing in a circus. Baucher's son Henri, quoted by General Decarpentry, tells us that his father "excelled at taking advantage of even the drawbacks of his horses" (**Baucher et son École**, p. 75, translation is mine). *Kleber* used to rear, so Baucher transformed his rearing into levades, which were probably not of great classical purity.

Gericault's training is more interesting. It was probably never very sophisticated, for the presentation Baucher did with this heretofore unrideable TB at the "Circus of the Champs Elysées" in Paris *only 27 days* after the horse was given to him was simple (although it comprised flying changes and pirouettes).

But here comes the interesting thing: General Decarpentry tells us that a staunch supporter of Comte d'Aure (Baucher's rival), Baron d'Etreillis, wrote, "After having brilliantly contributed to his master's glory, *Gericault* was sold to Monsieur de Moncoussin, *an average rider*, who used him for several years, with everyone in Paris' knowledge" (Op. cit., p. 60, translation is mine).

And this brings us to examining the second question: were these horses really *bad*, or were they *difficult?* There is a nuance. An excess of quality can lead a horse to restiveness if he is ever ill-ridden. Horses never fight if they don't have a good reason for it.

May I give a personal example? There was, in a riding school, a horse named *Carat* who was considered by the riders a true "terror," a dangerous horse. Part of his acting up was due to his incomprehension of what he was supposed to do. In other words, *Carat* could not be ridden by successive and different, as well as inexperienced, riders. He fought because he panicked. He needed *one* owner and rider.

He was then bought by Barbara Glasow, who is a national and international authority on therapeutic riding. That was a first step. A second step was achieved when he was given to me in training. I kept him one year (I am not Baucher!) and led him up to passing flying changes every third stride; I showed him at a NAHRA (North American for the Handicapped Riding Association) convention in Gladstone, NJ, and he returned to his owner. All this is no big feat.

But here comes my point. First, Barbara Glasow, who is herself physically very frail, bordering on incapacity, could not ride her horse for more than 10-15 minutes. She can now ride him as long as she pleases, because the horse is light to the legs and hands, and *no physical effort whatsoever is required* to ride him.

But there is more. She also uses the horse for sessions of therapeutic riding, which proves that the training has given *Carat* a wonderful psychological balance. *Carat* no longer panics.

The big discovery one makes when one starts studying and applying Baucherist techniques is that once light in hand, that is, relaxed and mobile in his lower jaw, a horse *becomes disciplined.* I cited the example of *Sweet William* in the previous chapter. I would like to mention an observation I have made: I do not have any problem administering any oral drug, a worming paste for instance, to my horses, and I attribute it to the fact that I work their mouth. A horse who is worked by means of flexions of the lower jaw also takes his bit much more freely, almost with pleasure when one tacks him. Last but not least, the flexion of the jaw fights *victoriously* the vice of passing the tongue over the bit.

For all their interest, these considerations have carried us away from our initial concern, namely the utility or non-utility of Baucherism for contemporary dressage competition. Let's come back to it.

After numerous years of riding "à la Baucher," I have come to the conclusion that lightness, that is, mobilization of the tongue as a prerequisite to *any* movement, can teach *any sound horse,* more or less rapidly (sometimes very fast), **some** of the High School movements, since collection is achieved much more rapidly (and in my view, much more *thoroughly*).

And collection is like the hat out of which the magician will draw successively a shawl, a rose, a rabbit, a book, etc... *But they never come in the same order.* One horse will give you great pirouettes (Andalusians, Lipizzans), another will be easy in the flying changes (Thoroughbreds), a third will passage (Anglo-Arabs), etc...

So what are we going to do when this happens? Are we going to take it, or leave it because it cannot be inserted into the FEI progression?

Chapter 12

How Does One Become a Baucherist?

I must admit to it; I am jealous of the late Colonel Alois Podhajsky, not because he was such a prestigious rider, not because he got the immense honor of being the head of the Conservatory of Equestrian Art which the Spanish Riding School of Vienna is, but because he found the most marvelous title that ever was for a riding book: **My Horses, My Teachers**. As a matter of fact, I've always felt that he robbed me of this title.

True, our horses are our best teachers, if we ever so little try to listen to them.

In 1978, the director of the French riding magazine *L'INFOR-MATION HIPPIQUE* I was working part-time for came to me with a surprising proposition: since we were regularly publishing interviews with professional riders, he offered me to publish one I would be the subject of.

"Very well," I answered, "but who is going to ask the questions?"

"Yourself. Who cares? Nobody has to know."

The prospect was only half pleasant. Of course, in the abstract, I was very excited at being both the interviewer and the interviewed. In fact, however, I felt that we were in some subtle manner lacking in respect to our readers. (And, as a matter of fact, the interview was never published.)

But here is my point: the first question I had imagined was:

"Jean-Claude Racinet, some say you are a Baucherist. What about it?"

And my answer would have been: "I do not know if I am a Baucherist, but I know my horses are."

Let us now take the matter by its beginning. I really cannot remember when I heard of Baucher for the first time. When did you first hear of Lucifer? Although never referred to openly, Baucher was omnipresent in the equestrian teaching of my youth, as some kind of somber myth, some ghostly figure like the statue of the Commander in Mozart's "Don Giovanni."

In 1953-54, as a first lieutenant, I attended a "Special Riding Course" at the Cavalry School of Saumur. We were a small bunch of lieutenants and captains, perhaps six or seven, with five horses each to ride every day, under the direction of Commandant (Major) de Saint-André, who was considered the best possible reference in the matter of French Classical Horsemanship. (Major de Saint-André would become the head of the "Cadre Noir" in 1964.)

Our five horses could be categorized as follows: a young horse, a jumper, an eventer, a dressage horse, and the fifth could belong to any of the above categories.

My dressage horse was named *Terrien*. He had been a mount of Commandant Margot, then the "Ecuyer-en-Chef" of the Cadre Noire. *Terrien* was a great teacher. When I was half-passing at a walk on the diagonal, if ever my seat did not stay where it should (that is, forward and on the inside seat bone), if, therefore, I would bring my weight on the outside seat bone, *Terrien* would simply shift from walk to canter, continuing his movement imperturbably on an unaltered trajectory.

Major Margot and Major de Saint-André were Baucherists, the

latter perhaps more than the former, but they probably would have died rather than admitting publicly to it. Major Margot had even fired one of his Equerries, Captain de Padirac (whose name will come up again in my story), reportedly because he caught him one day lifting the neck of his horse at a halt, according to Baucher's second "manner." At least, rumor had it.

This was the way at the Cavalry School at that time. Why was it so? If I were wicked—but I am a very good man—I would suggest that Baucherism would give the "Ecuyers-en-Chef" the edge they needed to overshine their subordinates, hence the interdiction for anyone else to "Baucherize." This could be done with a good conscience, since the interdiction ruled against Baucher in 1843 has never been lifted! Grandeur and Servitude of the Military! However bitter, duty is duty! Besides, one knows that Baucherism can be very dangerous as long as one has not reached a certain expertise (and by definition, a subordinate *never* attains expertise).

The example had been set long ago by the most prestigious "Ecuyer-en-Chef" of the French School, General (then Major) L'Hotte.

In the conclusion of the 12th edition of his **Méthode d'Equitation basée sur de nouveaux principes**, in 1864, Baucher wrote (translation is mine):

"The Army, as I have often said, has always had and always will have my liking. The dream of my whole life has been to make first its riders and then its equerries the best in Europe. I don't believe that God will allow me to see this realized, but I am confident. I know that truth always proceeds slowly and always comes out in the end.

Why should I not say it? It is the solace of my old age to see many high ranking personalities, many enlightened generals render justice to my principles. Each time that the name of some equestrian celebrity in the Army comes to my ears, I refer to my memories, because most often, I dare say almost always, this is one of my students, or at least a supporter of my method. They are those I see directing the equestrian teachings in the schools of the government. *As I am writing these lines, I happily hear that the command of the Manège of Saumur was just given to Major L'Hotte, who for 12 years honored me by asking for my advice and whose reputation cannot, rightfully, fear comparison with any other"* (op. cit. p. 212, italics are mine).

Poor Baucher! Hardly arrived in Saumur, Major L'Hotte took the following measures: 1) enforcement of the interdiction of Baucherism, an interdiction which had fallen into disuse; 2) interdiction of piaffe and passage with military horses.

So much for the faithful disciple.

This perhaps explains the kind of shame which always remained attached in the Army to the practice of Baucherism. An "Ecuyer en Chef" more "audacious" than his peers once stated: "One must practice Baucherism, but one must keep it secret."

General Decarpentry, incidentally, typifies this "shameful Baucherism." All in all, his book **Academic Equitation** is Baucherist. But surprisingly, each time Decarpentry comes up with Baucher, he apologizes, one way or another. One of my students had bought the book with high expectations; she was bitterly disappointed.

It is doubtful that this stigma attached to Baucher had anything to do with the gist of the matter, to wit Baucherism as such. The validity of his proceedings or his philosophy was not at stake, since his work had been extensively pilfered (so much so that many Baucherist concepts were apparent in the 1912 **Manuel d'Equitation**

et de Dressage, the rule book of the French Army). As a matter of fact, Baucher had challenged the "good society" of his time. Although a good half of this "good society" had sided with him at first, he had lost in the end the battle for "political correctness," and the "good society" had declared him "unbecoming." This judgement had been brought to Saumur by Count d'Aure in 1847, and since the officers of the Army, more so perhaps those of the Cavalry, were recruited from the ranks of the "good society," the anathema has survived.

This of course did not prevent the equerries of the Cadre Noir from having from time to time some bouts about Baucherism, but they had to do it in low key. Major de Saint-André (and Major Mazens, for instance) would sneak in their horse's stall at noon, and would nervously flex their horses' lower jaws, unbeknownst to the rest of the world—so they hoped—unbeknownst to their students, and unbeknownst to the dreadful *Ecuyer-en-Chef*, Commandant Margot, who probably himself...etc.

From time to time, new horses would show up in our horizon, most often fussy horses in want of a rider; they were sent to the "Special Riding Course." Thus, we were bequeathed a so-called *Petit Foc*, a grey horse who had been trained...and severely Baucherized...by Colonel Aublet, a former member of the Cadre Noir. (This was probably the last horse Col. Aublet had trained before he retired; at this time, he was no longer in the Manège of Saumur and free to train his horse as he pleased.)

Petit Foc was a real "problem horse": he was always at the passage, and we could not make him take any contact with the bit and trot normally. But *Petit Foc* would probably think that we were "problem riders," since we visibly were lacking the quiet seat necessary to ride such a horse. Major de Saint-André would teach us how to lower and extend the necks of our horses, not as a consequence of a flexion of the jaw but as a result of a confirmation of the contact by the rider's hand. This, of course, was 100 percent anti-Baucherist (our teaching was such a hodge podge!), and *Petit Foc*, who was a faithful, was not ready to accept it.

So Major de Saint-André would tell us: "Give me this horse, I'm going to show you." But after an hour of more and more furious efforts, he still had not persuaded *Petit Foc* of the virtues of the "lowering and extension of the neck!"

As I never missed an occasion to play the smart aleck, I asked Major de Saint-André to assign the horse to me. He stared at me in disbelief and annoyance and said: "You want it, you got it" (meaning: "but you better justify your pretension").

I don't remember that I did any better than anybody else with *Petit Foc*. In retrospect, and with all I know now, I can hardly understand how come we (and in the first place, our instructors) were so embarrassed with *Petit Foc*'s inextinguishable passage: there are many ways to prevent a horse from piaffing or passaging against his rider's will. The simplest was indicated by Baucher himself, i.e., the "effet d'ensemble."

Be that as it may, the case of *Petit Foc* was quite apt to confirm us in the (erroneous) opinion that a "Baucherized" horse could turn into an uncontrollable, infernal machine. As a matter of fact, that type of problem occurs only when the finesse of the horse outdoes that of the rider. The solution? Tirelessly cultivate the quality of one's seat. This is the snag with lightness: a horse who has been made light through his training will give you great joy, but he also at times will cruelly show you your limitations.

In **Academic Equitation** General Decarpentry gives us the

following warning: "It is possible to take a 'green' horse, and by confining him between four walls, to put him through a whole progression that would lead him to execute school airs within a relatively short time" (everyone will have recognized the "Baucherized" horse, but General Decarpentry doesn't elaborate further; he just lets us draw our own conclusion...). The horse "will appear to be schooled, but...will become intolerable in the open" (op. cit., English translation, J.A. Allen & Co., Ltd., London, 1971, p. 96).

And in a footnote, General Decarpentry adds: "One of the horses considered for inclusion in the French Olympic team in 1936 had been schooled in these conditions. In an attempt to make him usable out of doors, the owner entrusted him to a huntsman who used to ride him out hunting. At all the checks, and even at the meet, the horse would go into an interminable piaffer, and his unfortunate rider could do nothing to prevent this frenzy. The horse has never been cured of this vice, etc..."

General Decarpentry does not prove anything here, because to give such a horse to a huntsman is *exactly the thing not to do*. I do not know about the US, but in France, huntspeople are rather rough—not to say bad—riders.

Besides, General Decarpentry doesn't have much imagination. If such a horse was given to me, each time that he would piaffe against my will, I would drop the reins on one side and pull his head on the other side against my boot. One has never seen a horse, even "Baucherized," piaffe in this posture!

Moreover, this type of misfortune is not reserved for the "Baucherized" horse. In the French magazine *L'EPERON*, for September 1992, one could read on page 33, on the occasion of the Olympic Games in Barcelona: "During the awards ceremony for the

Dressage teams, *Gigolo* did not quit piaffing for a good ten minutes. So much so that it was becoming really grotesque!"

Now *Gigolo*, mount of the German rider Isabell Werth, Silver medalist individually, and Gold medalist with her team, had surely not been "Baucherized"! Or was he?

Back to your servant.

By the end of 1954, I was assigned to a regiment in Tunisia. France has just lost Indochina, and the other Dominions and Territories were to follow like dominos. When I arrived, the military operations were still very limited, and on the whole, the French settlers and the troops of Tunisia were still living at the nonchalant rhythm of colonial life. It was not without charm.

Colonel de Champvallier, who was commanding the cavalry of Tunisia (a few mounted troops, plus armored units) was somewhat the laughing stock of the young officers because of his extravagant riding habits. They would call him a "Beudantist" (and chuckle...). Colonel de Champvallier would spend interminable hours at a halt, the hands set high in order to elevate the horse's neck, deeply engrossed in some kind of meditation, waiting for lightness like a Zen monk longing for the "illumination." As a matter of fact, I have never seen Colonel de Champvallier on horseback otherwise than in this attitude.

Eight years later, I attended the courses of the "Staff College" in the Military School of Paris. There was a equestrian section (sport horses), and a show jumping team which I joined. Colonel de Champvallier had retired as a General, and as he was living in Paris, he was allowed to come and ride at the school. And lo and behold, the first time I saw him in the manège of the Military School, here he was, at a halt, his hand high, etc...

If by any chance a horse would start acting up because of the aggravation inherent to the type of service they were required, Captain Cottin, second in command of the equestrian section, would give it to him to fix up. Captain Cottin, who didn't understand in the least General de Champvallier's riding alchemy, would marvel at the good results the General would obtain with his meditative equitation. As for me, I thought the good results were probably due more to the cure of rest the horses had undergone.

Let us come back to Tunisia; It was the first time I heard of "Beudant." Somebody showed me his book **Main sans Jambes (Hand without Legs**, 1945); I browsed through it. I was very reserved about the lifting of the neck, but I liked very much the "hand without legs, legs without hand" concept, which in fact I had always practiced instinctively. The latter overcoming the former, I immediately became a supporter of Beudant, in spite of the mockery made of his principles by Colonel de Champvallier...and his staff officers.

Among them was a Captain—soon to be promoted to Major— by the name of de Padirac. I have already introduced my readers to him. Remember: he had been fired from the "Cadre Noir" upon having been caught by the "Ecuyer en Chef", Major Margot, as he was lifting his horse's head at a halt (at least, the rumor had it).

Most of de Champvallier's staff officers would practice "Beudant" just to humor their cantankerous boss. Without ignoring this latter advantage, Captain de Padirac was in addition certainly sincere.

Once, as Captain de Padirac had remained for a rather long time at a halt, raising his horse's head, I had found it funny to go past him on and on with my horse trotting with his nose literally on the ground. Perfectly aware of my little game, de Padirac squinted at me and simply said: "Racinet, your horse is working very well." I got the message. That was a very elegant way to have me come down one peg. It meant indeed: "Whereas you don't understand what I'm doing, I understand and even appreciate what you do. Your science is still too short to allow you any judgement."

Another day, in the early morning, Captain de Padirac did not notice my presence as I was watching him work his horse at a walk. It was a display of outstanding beauty: majesty on horseback. Superbly collected between the weight of the reins and the "wind" of the boot, his gray Barb was performing a splendid "school walk." Here also, there was a message. Certainly the lifting of the neck at a halt had not deteriorated this horse's gaits!

Sometime later, I had another and very determining experience. A French settler, Patrice de Warren, had given me a horse for training, or rather for retraining, because the horse, a "Selle Français," was very, very fussy. I had first had a tentative success by simply riding the horse with a full bridle on long reins and had placed second in my first show with a clear round. But soon the horse organized himself for a durable resistance, and my "rounds" were no longer "clear," but most often penalized with three faults (a refusal) or four faults (a pole knocked down). The fact was that the horse had a very bad relationship with the bit, any bit. He just couldn't suffer its presence in his mouth, and that would make him uneasy to ride, to say the least.

I had tried to come back to a soft snaffle, but without success. One day, as I was working on the flat and *Eliacin* (this was his name) was more particularly aggravated, I fell into a kind of calm rage. Since *Eliacin* was doing his best—or rather his worst—to avoid the contact with the bit, I decided to shorten progressively my reins, *without using my legs*, simply to make the beast "feel the steel," that is, acknowledge a steady contact with his tongue, the corners of the mouth, and the snaffle. *Eliacin* slowed—I maintained the contact; he stopped—I maintained the contact. He rolled his neck, completely overbent—I maintained the contact and thought I was winning when all of a sudden, in a snake-like movement, so quick that I could not analyze its "modus operandi," *Eliacin* collapsed his neck between his shoulders, and reversed completely the curvature thereof.

And then, *Eliacin* began slowly raising his head. I was completely puzzled, I did not know what to do, so I decided to stubbornly maintain the contact with my hand alone, and on short reins. Soon I could see *Eliacin*'s forehead between his ears; I raised my hand accordingly.

Now I ask my readers to visualize the picture; my horse all camped out, his neck vertical, his head above the horizontal, and me with my hands at the height of my eyes, my legs off the horse. What can happen in such a situation?

What happened this day was to mark me for the rest of my life. *Eliacin* could not *bear* the contact with the bit, but he was cornered, he had exhausted his possibilities of evasion, he had only one solution: try to jump *over* that bit. And suddenly, trembling with emotion, *Eliacin* started straight forward in a magnificent passage!

I kept the passage for a few seconds, perhaps ten, as long as I maintained the contact unaltered, then I opened my fingers, and *Eliacin* vented his anger in a furious gallop.

During all the process, I had not used my legs once.

This happening is interesting on two grounds. Passage calls for increased impulsion and increased balance. The first item had been produced by the contact with the bit, more so given the fact that *Eliacin* wanted furiously to *get rid* of it. This is a fascinating subject which opens fascinating perspectives, but I unfortunately cannot deal with it here since it would carry us too far away from our main subject.

As for the increase in balance, it was obvious to me that it had been supplied by the elevation of the neck.

So I decided that I would try, as soon as possible, to start the training of a horse by raising his head and neck at a halt, in a quest for the Grail in my turn, like Colonel de Champvallier's ilks.

This occasion was given to me shortly thereafter, as I was assigned to a unit in Algeria. The only horse I could grab there was a four-year-old Barb, rather tall for his breed (16.1). For whichever reason, I didn't like him (although he was to become one of my best horses ever). This gave me the courage to engage into unknown and possibly dangerous grounds.

My apprehensions can be understood. With *Eliacin*, I had not raised the head of the horse, he had done it in order to escape my demand for contact. But now, I had to do it myself, and I did not know exactly why and how. I was so afraid of my responsibility that in the meantime, as I was investigating this new procedure, I also would teach my horse to lower and extend his neck at an energetic trot. This required two different types of fingering, but Barbs are intelligent. *R'mel* never got confused.

Here I have to place some incidental information about the Barb. Many Americans, when they hear the word "Barb," think of the so-called Spanish Barb, not knowing that the "Barb" is the horse of North Africa. The "Spanish" Barb is the supposed descendant of supposed Barbs supposedly bred by the Spaniards and supposedly introduced on this continent by the "conquistadors." The Spanish Barb is a supposition; the Barb is a reality. End of parenthesis.

Now, about the results: My horse *R'mel* learnt how to passage and canter in place in such a short time that I hardly dare being more explicit, lest I be called a kidder. Want to know more? Two weeks, believe it or not. I was so stunned myself that this is about all the "High School" tricks I required from my horse. Besides, I just wanted *R'mel* to be a jumper, and he turned out to be an excellent one, probably partly because of his training on the flat.

The lifting of the horse's neck alone, however, does not make one a Baucherist for so much. Some other masters tried it too, in the first place the German Seeger who happened to be one of the most peevish enemies of Baucher. Still, at the time, I was persuaded that I had found *the* equestrian truth, the absolute weapon, the A-bomb of horsemanship. Since then, I have met other riders overflowing with the same enthusiasm for the same reason, and my relative coolness as compared to their excitement may have made me look like a wet blanket to their eyes.

Back in Europe after seven years in a row spent in North Africa, I found that with our bony, massive, and a tad stiff jumpers, this proceeding which had worked marvelously with a supple north African Barb, although still very valuable, was not the alpha and omega. I was on a quest for *something else,* something *more.*

This something more was to be the flexion of the lower jaw. It crept surreptitiously into my mind, and I cannot link the growing awareness I got of its necessity to some specific event. But I have kept a vivid memory of a gentleman riding in the forest of Chantilly, east of Paris. I myself was riding in the same lane with a lady friend of mine. As we were going in opposite directions, we went past each other and greeted each other with urbanity, as is the rule between riders. He was cantering calmly with a horse in a superb carriage, on

[171]

looped reins, deep into the saddle, and with his legs vertical, immobile, and relaxed. The horse was gently foaming at the mouth. The whole picture would give an impression of balance, softness, and mastery. A picture worthy of admiration.

"Who is this gentleman?," I asked my friend. "Oh, some old weirdo," she answered.

This is to be paralleled by the following, drawn from André Monteilhet's **Les Maîtres de l'Oeuvre Equestre (The Masters of the Equestrian Work)**. Speaking of Armand Charpentier, deceased in 1948, one of the last known (and renowned) Baucherists, he writes: "He had seen great Baucherists, when following a hunt, for instance, set their horses at a medium canter through an 'effet d'ensemble' followed with a release of hand and legs, and their horses would canter like this for miles, keeping their balance without the help of their riders' aids" (Op. cit., p. 77, English translation is mine).

A bunch of weirdos, as we see.

I bit the bullet on this matter with *Tarzan*, who was to be my last Army horse. He had been assigned to me when I was in the Military School of Paris, and he had followed me to my last garrison as a sport horse. *Tarzan* had been a glory of the military jumping grounds, but he was getting old and cantankerous. A small horse, his generosity had been used and abused, and if I wanted to take advantage of the remnant of the spark that could stay in him, I had to ride him by the millimeter: he would not forgive any error. Heretofore, *Tarzan* had been used, exploited. To use the terms of Baucher, one had contended oneself to exploit his instinctive forces, to give them a direction. Now he needed to be **"dressé,"** that is, **trained**. He needed collection. And since I was not ready, in order to get it, to push onto the bit, a thing which I had always despised, I contrived this simple technique I call the "impulsive flexion," which I have always used successfully since. Make the jaw yield with the hand alone and then push forward. In other words, instead of pushing onto the bit, push onto lightness.

By systematically associating lightness and forward movement, I also countered any setting behind the bit subsequent to the flexion of the lower jaw, which in my mind I didn't doubt the possibility of, since I was brainwashed, like everybody else.

As a matter of fact, I would establish in the years to follow that this danger is null, it does not exist: the flexion of the jaw is *by itself* impulsive, since it creates relaxation, hence balance, hence facilitates impulsion.

I retired shortly thereafter and set myself about making a living as a professional rider. With the first horse I taught how to passage, as a civilian, I did it by means of impulsive flexion. It came very soon.

I have since used this technique as a base for my training, and it has never let me down. Of course, it is not a magic wand, and the progress is sometimes slow. But I am convinced it would be slower without the seeking for the mobility of the jaw. I have tried, several times, to do without it, and *always* have been obliged to come back to it.

Does this make a Baucherist out of me? I think so, since I hold that the whole work of Baucher was nothing else than a slow, progressive setting into evidence of the relaxation of the horse's jaw as the main tool for balance. This is the fundamental discovery of Baucher. I even think that if Baucher, by the end of his life, would lift his horse's head and neck, it was out of a desire for a better mastery of the horse's jaws.

Let me quote one more time Andre Monteilhet, about Armand

[173]

Charpentier.

"Charpentier devotes to Baucher about 60 pages stuffed with utterly instructive anecdotes, some of them heretofore little known, like that about *Bienfaisant*, a young horse 'without vice nor virtue,' bought in a fair in Le Havre, who would oppose, for weeks, 'an overwhelming force of inertia to all the suppling exercises Baucher would submit him to.' One day, tired of it, Baucher stopped in the center of the manège, holding the reins in the left hand. All of a sudden, he felt that the resistance has vanished. Immense discovery, for Baucher, that the first resistances consist in the contraction of the jaw, and that the relaxation thereof entails the suppleness of the neck. Other discovery: the fixed position of the hand, the efficacy of which he just had acknowledged and which was to be the last thought ("always this, never that") he told again to L'Hotte who had come to visit him on his deathbed" (Op. cit., p. 77, English translation is mine).

This experience happened at the beginning of Baucher's career, before he went to Paris. One can find it narrated by Baucher himself in the 13th edition of his "complete works" (1867). Baucher concludes the episode with these words: "So started the Method." This statement is together understandable and surprising. It is understandable because of the date on which it was issued: 1867, five years before Baucher's death.

But it is also surprising because one knows that the flexion of the jaw as the fundamental prerequisite to any other flexion was not present in the beginning of the Method. It is as if Baucher, after having acknowledged the importance of the discovery, had stacked it in a corner of his mind, where it slept for some time before coming back in a stronger and stronger manner, up to becoming the central part of the Method.

So Baucher is right in saying "the method was born," but he should have added "although I was not fully aware of it."

Be that as it may, this permanent lightness of the jaw, better obtained in his second "manner" than in his first, would allow Baucher to define an effortless riding style based on the release of the aids, their separated wielding and their moderation, the horse being left in "liberty on parole" as long as there is no need for a transition.

It also led Baucher to a collection which resembles strangely that of the old school as far as balance is concerned, but with less stress borne upon the flexion of the hocks, since Baucher did not practice the airs above the ground.

So all in all, what is it exactly, to be a Baucherist?

In my opinion, it is first to practice a riding style abiding by the principles of release, separation, and moderation of the aids. And as far as the training of the horse is concerned, it is to refuse, ever, any compromise with the balance of the horse, at the cost of possibly limiting one's demands in the beginning as concerns movement.

Procedures are not important; they may vary, and we even may find some new ones which Baucher didn't think of. But philosophy matters, and the Baucherist philosophy is: balance creates movement, and not the other way around.

Chapter 13

A Letter To Susan

O n occasion of an article I wrote in the series on Baucher in the "old" *DRESSAGE & CT* magazine, which is at the origin of this book, I received a letter from which I quote the following excerpts:

"My hope is that in one of your upcoming articles, you would talk more about how, for example, you ask for flexion of the jaw, especially without pulling. It seems you inadvertently keep it quite a mystery. I am sure you don't mean it to be so, but I think you have a lot of followers through this magazine sitting on the edges of their chairs wondering what to do.

"I have ridden a few times with a person who said she was versed in the French way. She had me bend my horse's head left and right. Yes, I got submission, but he was not happy. I was definitely pulling on the reins, not backwards of course, but left and right. I never made the connection that perhaps this was 'Baucherism'. And if you are able to get flexion at the jaw, how does this connect to the rest of the horse's body, i.e., raising the back and incorporating all the muscles of the topline?"

Here is my answer.

Dear Susan,

Let me first come back to the question: "How does the flexion of the jaw connect with the rest of the horse?"

The matter, as I have said, is far from fully investigated, probably because of the misgivings of many a rider about the technique, and also because of the fact that the vets (who have the necessary anatomical knowledge) most often don't ride (and amongst those who ride, we would have to find a Baucherist, which further reduces the odds).

In Chapter 7 of this book I have quoted Mrs. Nicholson, of Miami University in Oxford, OH, who stresses the importance of the "sterno-hyoid" system, which links the tongue to the sternum.

A horse, as I have tirelessly stressed, doesn't have any collar bone. The spine and rib cage are somewhat "floating" between the shoulder blades. When one rides a horse, his size diminishes. This, of course, entails some troubles.

One of these troubles could be a tension in this "sterno-hyoid" system, brought about by the lowering of the sternum due to the pressure of the rider's weight. In other words, it is possible that the simple fact of being ridden creates a tension in the horse's mouth. Relieving this tension by means of relaxing exercises would in turn induce the sternum to rise and in so doing make the horse's back take in charge his rider's weight.

This supposition is mine. It calls for further examination. It is a fact that if by any chance one rides one's horse with a close contact saddle, one can feel some muscles of the back move under one's seat at the very moment a horse gives a deep flexion of the jaw.

Baucher would simply state that since the resistances of a horse kind of "buttress" against each other and end up in the horse's mouth, suppressing this last link is likely to destroy, at least momentarily, the whole chain.

And after all, this reasoning makes some sense.

Let us come into more details:

The flexion of the jaw is never asked for by an alternate traction on the reins, left, right, left, right, entailing a swinging movement of the head. This is German riding and aims at working the poll directly without acting on the jaw first. For whatever reasons, the Germans want to avoid the yielding of the jaw.

I have, I think, explained well enough in my articles that the notion of "flexion" of the jaw evolved considerably in the course of Baucher's life, from a simple "munching" of the bit occasioned by the lateral flexions of the neck to a "yielding" of the jaw alone obtained only with the fingers, a yielding that should obligatorily precede the arching of the poll and neck and be the condition thereof.

By the way, the flexions of the neck it is about were made at a halt (nothing to do with the alternate tractions on the reins with a horse in motion of the German method). I described these flexions in Chapter 3, and I reproduced the drawings of Baucher's "Method," 12th edition.

These lateral and direct flexions of the neck and poll were first meant to create the "ramener" (i.e., the classical head set with the poll the highest point and the forehead perpendicular), which was the main condition, in Baucher's mind, for balancing the horse at all gaits. The chomping at the bit was secondary to those neck flexions and a kind of proof that they had been correctly waged.

Then Baucher changed this order and placed the stress first and foremost on the flexion of the jaw, promoted in turn to the rank of "golden key" to achieve balance; the flexions of the neck became mere ways to achieve this flexion of the jaw. They were simplified accordingly; the angle of the lateral flexions dwindled, and the direct

[179]

neck flexion disappeared in time, with an important exception, which is the "ramener outré" (outright overbending) of the second "man-ner" (which, as a matter of fact, is a way to isolate the flexion of the jaw by saturating the possibility of the horse's evading by flexing the neck).

So by and large, in the second method, the head is elevated to insure that the neck will not bend first and the flexion of the jaw asked alone, at a halt first and later at a very slow walk and trot.

When the jaw yields, the rider lowers his hands, lengthens his reins somewhat, and lets the head take a position nearing the vertical. The reins are then loose, so the head cannot come behind the vertical.

The flexion of the jaw is the mean. The purpose of it is to achieve the yielding of the jaw (end of the resistances of force), which is acted out through the mobility of the jaw.

When the horse is fully trained, the mobility of the jaw should come about upon the mere half-tension of one rein or both.

This mobility of the jaw is the proof of its relaxation, which in turn entails the relaxation of the neck, shoulders, and even back of the horse.

The relaxation in turn fosters balance, for the very simple reason that if there were no balance, there would be contractions.

If a horse can be kept in a permanent state of relaxation of his jaw, he is kept in a permanent state of balance. Baucher called it "balance of the first genre."

So what exactly is the flexion or mobilization of the jaw and how should it be obtained?

As I explained in Chapter 7, the flexion of the jaw cannot be practiced if one has not been introduced to it by a teacher. I will, however, try to do my best to make it better understood.

If you have a kitten at your home, take it in your arms, turn it on its back, belly up, and with the thumb and index of your left hand, for instance, press gently and progressively if needed the two corners of the cat's mouth. All of a sudden, the cat will open its mouth widely and stick its tongue out; then he will bring his tongue in and shut his mouth. You have here a good approximation of what the flexion of the jaw is (you have to quit pressing as soon as the mouth opens).

The flexion of the jaw should entail the mobility of the tongue (up and down), making the bits jingle; the relaxation of the jaw and the mobility of the tongue up to its fixation under the horse's poll entail the relaxation of the poll and that of the first third of the neck at least.

Now you will notice that all the resistances of the horse created by the imbalance or creating it are primarily manifested by a tension of the front third of the neck. By "locking" this area, the horse can ignore the orders of his rider, disengage his hindquarters, and do what he pleases. He can even swindle you by displaying a magnificent, so-called "classical" head set (always a tad too low, though) devoid of any relaxation.

Incidentally, we can see that all the formal requirements on the position of the head and neck, as well as the position of the rider, are futile, since relaxation, and not forced posture, is the name of the game. The position of the horse's head, as well as that of his rider, should proceed from relaxation.

This is why, in Baucher's second "manner," the relaxation of the mouth demanded as a rule by the hand alone, the neck being fully developed upwards, is the absolute prerequisite to any movement. Subsequently, the diverse occurrences of the riding process, the diverse exercises, will progressively push the horse's body toward his poll in a constantly maintained relaxation.

Now, since the lateral flexions of the poll and neck (at a halt) are only meant to induce the mobility of the jaw, one can imagine that it should be possible after a while to dispense with them, i.e., to ask for this jaw mobility directly.

This brings us to emphasize the notion of fixed hand.

For a horse, clenching his teeth is a natural precaution against the possible roughness of his rider's hand. One can imagine that he will be very reluctant to abandon this defense. This is why, by the slightest manifestation of yielding, he should receive an instantaneous, automatic reward through the release of the hand action.

For this, the hand should act through a mere pressure of the fingers on the reins without any pulling from the arms, and this is why:

There are two types of hand action: the "drawer" action and the "lemon" action. The "drawer" action is what one does to open a drawer; if the drawer is clogged and yields all at once, one is likely to fall back. The "lemon" action is what we do when pressing a lemon. If the lemon resists and then yields all at once, nothing big will happen; one has never seen anyone fall by squeezing a lemon.

As a rule, on horseback, the action of hand should follow the pattern: "drawer...lemon." The first action is a "drawer" type action, meant to confirm the contact with the bit. The following action is a "lemon" type action, meant to obtain the yielding of the jaw.

The error would be to do "drawer...drawer," that is to say, to pull strongly with the arms when the resistance occurs.

On the contrary, if a soft "drawer" type action has not brought about the mobility of the jaw (this happens only when the horse is fully trained), the "lemon" type action should be used to overcome the resistance.

In both cases—drawer and lemon—a traction is applied. But in the first case, the rider is absolutely incapable of mastering this traction, i.e., to "yield" when the horse's mouth itself yields. Why? Because the human reflexes are "too slow." It is not a question of good will; it is a simple physiological datum.

For instance, try this little game. Take a one dollar bill and let it hang vertically between another person's open thumb and index finger. The bill is half engaged between the person's fingers, which should be at least one inch apart. Then drop the bill; the other person will never grab it. This shows the limits of human reflexes.

The eyes of the person see the bill start its fall; it takes a fraction of a second for the mind to realize it. Then it takes another fraction of a second for the brain to send an order to the muscles, and another fraction of a second for the muscles to move. All these minute delays add up to perhaps half a second, during which the bill has fallen too great a distance to be grabbed.

This shows that the reward of the horse, as he yields, should not depend on the rider's good will but should happen automatically. This automaticity is realized by the "lemon" type action. In this type of action, the fingers squeeze the reins in place, "convulsively if needed" (Beudant), as if the action was targeting the rein itself and not the horse's mouth.

This is what "fixed hand" means; if upon the horse's yielding, your hand has moved back, ever so slightly, you were "pulling" with the arm. The "fixed hand" is not a hand which is simply fixed with respect to the horse's mouth (that is, avoids involuntary movements); this is a quality of the rider's seat. A "fixed hand" is not a *hand which is fixed with respect to the horse's back, since it would probably "lock in" the horse and make him pull in turn.*

The "fixed hand" is a hand which is fixed with respect to itself, i.e., which does not offer any recoil as the horse's mouth yields.

This fixicity is very difficult to acquire, and this is why Baucherism can only be taught to confirmed riders. Another reason for Baucherism to be reserved to experienced riders is that once the horse is light, you can no longer balance off the reins, lest you destroy lightness and considerably aggravate your horse. I have seen horses who were trained to lightness and later ridden by heavy and awkward riders become literally enraged and charge like bison when cantering. A horse who has given himself to his rider thanks to lightness, if ill-ridden subsequently, feels he was taken advantage of, violated, and then it will become much more difficult, not to say impossible, to convince him back into lightness. I often tell my students (and I mean it): "If you are not or have never been capable in your life of jumping a 3'6" fence with your hands behind your back, forget about High School riding."

To apply the principle of the "fixed hand," one should hold the reins differently from what is taught in the German riding style. In this style, the rider constantly has all of his/her fingers closed on the reins.

In the other style (lightness), the reins are primarily held by the "pincer" thumb-index (the thumb applying by its tip onto the rein), and the reins are adjusted in length without the intervention of the other fingers. Then, when the reins are carefully adjusted in this way, the other fingers are gently "posed" on the reins, in an ajar position, so that the hand can give more (by opening) or take more (by closing). This gives three "nuances" for the action of the hand, which can "give" (opening), "resist" (fingers ajar), or "act" (fingers closed).

These three nuances were first defined by La Guérinière (1688-1751), to whom the German School likes to refer, in my view in a "lip service" manner. La Guérinière defines "la main légère" ("the light hand," give), "la main douce" ("the soft hand," resist), and "la main ferme" ("the firm hand," act).

A good way to acquire the good position of hands is to ride with two crops, one in each hand, and to make sure that no matter what, regardless of the actions of hands one is called on to do, they remain strictly vertical, i.e., hanging constantly in front of the rider's knee. (In the beginning, have somebody check on you and yell at you each time one of these crops quits the vertical line, which will be quite often!)

To describe the same position, Nuno Oliveira would evoke a rider having one lighted candle in each hand.

And now, let's be very practical. I suppose you are the good rider I have described who does not establish her balance off the reins or by squeezing her legs. How are you going to ask for your first flexions of the jaw? Here is a simplified method.

Mouth your horse with a snaffle, not a thick, hollow one but a "French" snaffle, or a Dr. Bristol, or the cheapest snaffle they use in Western Riding. Use no noseband, or a loose one.

On foot, face the horse, place your thumbs in the rings of the snaffle, and push very progressively (no jolts) upward and in a slanted way, toward the corners of the mouth. The horse will open his mouth and probably move his lower jaw from side to side. Don't yield as long as this happens. Then, the horse will move his tongue up and down, the lower jaw remaining in a median position. Immediately (and even if you don't feel any particular yielding, your tact will develop later on) drop the rings completely and let the horse's head take a normal position. You will observe that the horse then "chomps his bit" (I hate this expression; I use it for want of a better one, but what we look for is a real and deep relaxation of the jaw, as if the horse were swallowing his saliva—and he probably is).

Prevent the horse from backing. If you can't, do this exercise in the horse's stall.

When this exercise is well understood by both rider and horse, try to push the snaffle softly toward the bars of the lower jaw. You will find more resistance. Drop the bit at the first hint of yielding. If the horse has really yielded, he should "masticate" the bit several times with a calm look in his eyes. If he makes the bit "jingle," even better.

Then ride the horse and at a halt try to get the same sensations from horseback. Remember: don't pull at all. Squeeze your fingers "convulsively if needed," but beforehand, adjust the reins tightly, your fingers being ajar. You must feel the mouth, although your fingers remain ajar (crop vertical).

As soon as you get one flexion, drop the reins completely. Pat your horse.

The method described here is simple. Later on, you may mouth the horse with a full bridle and try the flexions of Baucher. But remember: the goal is not the opening of the mouth (although the mouth has to open) but its relaxation. The opening of the mouth alone is no proof of relaxation, as we all know when we go to the dentist's. In this respect, there are horses who resist not by clenching but by gaping the mouth. You would then have to adjust the noseband a little tighter, and at any rate as tight as required to deprive the horse of this possibility of evasion.

[186]

What about the legs? Use them only if the horse backs up, and try to get the flexion by the hand alone. It is possible to get flexions of jaw, the hand resisting, by a "pinching" of the spurs (beware: no "jabbing"). However, this should not be the usual way of obtaining the flexion of the jaw; you would end up constantly using your spurs.

Another very important practical detail: don't wear gloves, and don't use braided reins. In this type of riding, it is very important to be able to let the reins slide, ever so slightly, between the fingers from time to time and especially when the horse has given you a yielding of the jaw. Your hand should never offer a strong barrier that can only offend or numb the horse's mouth.

Since with braided reins, it is difficult to use one's fingers, one is tempted to pull with one's arms; as a matter of fact, it is their purpose: to help the rider pull. Now pulling with the arms to overcome a horse is proof of the impotence of the rider. If you pull, your horse will pull in turn, and he will win. When you slow a horse, stop, or rein back (very important), your hands should not move one millimeter back. With a horse accustomed to bolting away, if I were given the choice between braided reins and slick reins, I would choose slick reins.

Many riders don't understand that the lack of intelligence, the rudeness, and the coarseness of their hands aggravate their horses or make them lose their balance. If you use coarse reins, your horsemanship will be coarse.

The horse of one student I met in a clinic was "jigging" constantly; I tried to explain to her that the horse was jigging against her hands, but she would not believe me, since her hands were perfectly still. Sure, they were. So I had her practice the following exercise: for no special reason, just to play, constantly change the length of the reins. She did, and immediately the horse stopped jigging.

I would also draw your attention to the necessity of changing your riding habits before you start working on the flexion of the jaw. You first have to make sure that you practice the "release of the aids," that is to say that, systematically, you disengage your aids as soon as their order has been executed by the horse. This is more particularly important for your legs; quit pushing onto the bit! Your legs should be totally inactive as long as there is no need for a transition (acceleration) or a specific cue (flying change, canter departure, etc.), in which case your cue should be as "punctual" as possible. Even in a lateral movement, your outside leg should not be "glued" to the horse, but release its pressure as soon as the horse starts moving laterally.

Riding in lightness is a whole: you cannot take a part of it and make a hodge podge, the American way (there is no "melting pot" in horsemanship), with other techniques inspired by different philosophies.

You cannot introduce the flexion of the jaw into a forceful style of riding; you would end up practicing the worst of the first "manner" of Baucher. More than a set of techniques, lightness is a frame of mind. You must be imbued with the necessity of the release of the aids (the aids ask, restore, transform; they never maintain), the separation of the aids (hand without legs and vice versa and, even more demanding, the use of one rein at a time), and the moderation of the aids (soft actions of legs, short actions of hands).

This re-education takes time. Start it now. And don't do it alone; ask some friend to yell at you each time the old reflexes resurface.

Many believe that these wonderful principles are only niceties to be practiced, as a kind of final touch, with the almost fully trained horse; nothing could be more erroneous. Lightness is a contract that we propose to the horse from the very beginning of our training and every minute of said training. By this contract, we tell the horse: "I have given you the orders in the most polite and appropriate way possible; now you do the job, while I rest."

"On horseback," Nuno Oliveira would say, "one should rest and not struggle."

When I was still in France, I would introduce my students to the flexion of the jaw only when I felt they were really advanced in their training and had a good perception of the horse's balance. I had an "aristocratic" conception of the teaching of horsemanship. And this was the right way. Since the flexion of the jaw is a kind of "initiation," it had to be given only when the student was prepared to receive it.

But in the US, given the huge distances and the fact that the clinician sometimes sees his pupils only twice a year, one is obliged to release much more information at once, hoping that the student will make good use of it.

So the responsibility, Susan, is yours; the ball is in your court. If the technique doesn't work for you, don't incriminate the technique; carefully try to determine where you have parted from the indications I have given in this letter.

The flexion of the jaw cannot really be learnt from a book, since it is about a feeling, and feelings cannot be shared or transmitted. People who have never experienced a migraine cannot understand what it really is. They can only guess. Thus in the past, many a grave disease was blamed on the patient's self-pity.

Even if I were physically present when you ride, I could not

make you feel what I feel when I get the relaxation of the jaw. I would
have to be a ghost, place my hands in yours, and make you exactly
feel what it is like when the mouth yields.

And I measured my responsibility as I was about to deliver all
this information in this letter and in my articles. I know that any
misuse that will be made of the technique will be put on the score of
the method itself. All the more so since "tact" is involved in the
matter. You may take piano lesson after piano lesson and yet never
become a great pianist. Musicality cannot be taught. I know some
great sport riders who cannot get a real flexion of the jaw. They
"pull;" it's in their genes.

The same probably applies to German riding, as stands out, for
instance, from the haze surrounding the notion of "half-halt," or that
of "permeability," or that of "forward movement." They cannot be
understood by the book only. They have to be "felt."

The advantage of German riding, however, is that it is widely
exposed; it has many trainers, teachers, and performers and, at the
top, great artists who can show the best of it (although I am not saying
that all those at the top are great artists; some are real laborers).

Baucherism, or, to use a more general term, riding in lightness,
does not possess this advantage. Even when Nuno Oliveira was still
alive, one had to go to Portugal to see him or be lucky enough to
attend one of his rare clinics. (The poor man had to travel the world
over and save enough time to train his horses at home, and when
one considers that many of these horses, talented as they might have
been, were performing all the High School movements, one wonders
how he could stand the pace. And, as a matter of fact, he didn't.)

If we want to save this "riding in lightness," we will have to
someday create a "Baucherist University" which will form instruc-

tors who will in turn spread across this country.

I throw out this idea as one casts a bottle into the sea.

Sincerely,

Appendix 1

Was Baucher Right?

Baucherism can easily be summed up. It is based on three assumptions.

- The first is that balance comes prior to movement, and not the other way around.

- The second is that balance can be obtained, and therefore improved, at a halt.

- The third is that the mobility of the lower jaw, which Baucher calls lightness, is the guarantee for balance in action.

Let's examine these assumptions one by one.

The first assumption is just what it is: an assumption. It cannot be proven. It certainly makes sense, and may appeal to some (including myself). However, to prove the truth of it, one would have to train a horse in this way, and then erase this training and train *the same horse* in the other way. This, of course, is impossible. Moreover, if this were possible, one would have to repeat the operation with a sufficient number of horses so as to acquire a statistical certainty.

Still, experience shows that, however carefully broken down the progression of the training, most horses don't have the innate intelligence to adapt spontaneously their balance to the requirements of the exercise they are asked to perform. For the bulk of it, this balance has to be realized beforehand, *and then* probably the exercise *fine tunes* it.

But what is going to militate strongly in favor of this first assumption is *the absolute truth of the second*. Because if balance can be obtained easily at a halt, why bother to engage in a long and fastidious progression of movements? This second assumption is easily demonstrable.

The "motor" of a horse—everybody will agree on that—is for the main in his hind legs, whose pendulum movement creates the necessary forward thrust. This pendulum movement hinges round the coxo-femoral joint, i.e., the junction between the femur and the pelvis.

Although this "hinge" is not absolutely fixed with respect to the horse's body—it moves to and fro at a walk or trot due to the alternating rotation of the croup by each step or stride—it stands to reason that the more forward the general position of this point is, the more the "engine" will work *under the mass* rather than behind it, and therefore the more balance there will be.

Hence realizing the balance is nothing else than forwarding this point to a maximum, by "tipping under" the pelvis, and this can certainly be studied at a halt. For this, in his first manner, Baucher would use the "effet d'ensemble", whose possible drawbacks we mentioned in this book. In his second manner, he would use the "mise en main", i.e., "bringing in hand", a combination of neck lifting and yielding of the jaw, meant to create the perfect "ramener", on the "weight of the reins". "Mise en main" would be obtained by the hand alone, the role of the legs reduced to a mere indication to "go".

It has to be observed that this ideal balance can be realized only inasmuch as the horse can *physically* achieve a *thorough* tipping under of his pelvic bones. We shall come back to this question later.

What about the third assumption (lightness as a guarantee of the conservation of balance in action)? Here again, no measurement can be done, one has to rely to mere observation. Now experience has shown me, time and again, that if the lightness of the jaw does not give one immediately the total, perfect balance, it gives one *the best possible balance* a horse can afford at a given point in time. Each time I have tried to abstain from demanding it, the results have been lesser, and I have been obliged to come back to using it.

Now what are the obstacles which lie between the best possible balance of the moment and the best possible balance as such, that is, the ideal balance, the "equilibrium of the first genre" of Baucher second "manner"? Are they due to the stiffness of some muscles, in which case they could be overcome progressively? I don't think so. I think that while the lightness of the jaw gives one the best possible balance a horse can afford at a given point in time, this balance *is not going to perfect itself,* whichever amount of good horsemanship one may subsequently come up with, as long as one has not addressed the real problems.

These real problems, Baucher could hardly have had any idea of, although it is possible he had a *vague intuition* of them, which would be enough to make him a genius. They lie in the vertebral blockings and other joint subluxations (sacroiliac for instance), to which any horse will be subject in his life span.

I have myself become aware of these vertebral "blockings" by reading the book of Dr. Giniaux **Les Chevaux m'ont dit (What the horses have told me)**, which I translated into English for Xenophon Press. I happen to know personally Dr. Giniaux; he taught me the way to "erase" these blockings, at the level of the brain, where they originate, through a specific type of manipulation (which is not a "chiropractic", but rather an "osteopathic" manipulation; I will elaborate on that further in this appendix).

What I have found out is that

- all the horses are subject to vertebral "blockings",
- no yielding of the jaw can liberate these blockings; they require a specific manipulation,
- when a horse is reasonably rid of vertebral "blockings", then the flexion of the jaw becomes *utterly possible,* and with a simple snaffle to boot. I even consider it the litmus test, the proof that the horse's physical problems have been solved.

This, which shows the limits of Baucherism, also comes as a glaring justification of it, because as soon as the vertebral problems are solved, the "mise en main" can be obtained *at once,* the ideal balance, that is, the "equilibrium of the first genre" of Baucher second "manner", with a total lifting of the withers and a subsequent total tipping under of the pelvis, can be obtained *at once,* and the main difficulties of High School, piaffe, passage, canter pirouettes, and flying changes in short sequences can be overcome in *a few weeks* (piaffe, and sometimes passage, can be obtained immediately, at least in their principle).

Now one question arises: if it is true that all horses display vertebral blockings which come athwart of the real balance, and which have been heretofore unknown and therefore untreated, how come that the Masters of yore achieved wonderful trainings? How come that some horses reach the Grand Prix level every year, some of them brilliantly?

A first part of the answer is that these wonderful trainings have been achieved with *gifted horses*. What is a gifted horse? A horse who through physical soundness, added to a good share of luck, escapes the most crippling vertebral blockings. It is also a horse who can, in part, work *around* his physical limitations, as have done the true athletes of all times.

The skill of the trainers would account for the rest. It is possible that Baucher, due to the power of his proceedings, to wit strong attacks with the spurs to "enclose" the horse, effet d'ensemble, etc... may have forced some of his horses to perform *in spite of* their possible vertebral limitations; hence the character of artificiality of some of his performances, the general aspect of "mournful resignation" of some of his mounts.

It is also possible, almost certain, that Baucher at least in his first manner and unbeknownst to himself, would liberate some blockings in the cervical vertebrae, through his lateral flexions of the neck. For instance, a progressive and as thorough as possible lateral bending of the neck on the "stiff" side, without any rotation of the line of the ears (the head remaining perpendicular to the ground) may *unlock a C7 or a T1,* with spectacular results upon the ability of the horse to raise his withers and move his shoulders.

But if a horse was afflicted with a blocking of the second cervical vertebra, for instance, which creates pains and aches in the poll and jaw muscles, no amount of flexion of the lower jaw could have solved the problem; the horse would have clattered his teeth in pain (modern "Dressage" takes care of the matter with a tight drop nose band, which is worse).

The great Masters were known through the success of their trainings; but no one knows about the horses they did not succeed with. Nobody ever knew their names. In the light of what we know now, it is absolutely impossible that they might have succeeded with certain horses afflicted with severe vertebral problems. For instance, Beudant speaks of a horse called *Conspirateur* who, in the 23rd

Dragoons then under the command of Colonel Faverot de Kerbrech, was practically impossible to ride, because of his rearing habits. Colonel Faverot de Kerbrech had the horse trained by some of his officers, under his instructions, according to the teachings of Baucher second manner. The rearings were overcome with the "effet d'ensemble on the spur", and a strict application of "hand without legs, legs without hand" did the rest. This was, says Beudant, a revelation for all the officers of the 23rd Dragoons.

But honestly Beudant is obliged to admit that *Conspirateur* remained difficult to ride", and that the veterinarian of the Regiment had him undergo surgery for a supposed "intestinal fungus". We are not told of the results of this operation upon the behavior of the horse.

Nowadays, we would diagnose that *Conspirateur* was afflicted with a serious blocking of the "atlas" (C1), probably linked to an L6 (last lumbar) and S1 (first sacral) problem. Baucher himself would not have got the better of him.

Baucher theorized that all the "resistances" support each other, forming a "chain" which ends up in the horse's mouth. Therefore, by relaxing the mouth, one would at least momentarily suppress the resistances, one would "give them their leave". This theory loses much of its appeal in front of the new discoveries in the pathology of the vertebral column I am mentioning here, since isolate flexions of the lower jaw will release a vertebral blocking only by chance.

But this partial disavowing of Baucher's theory certainly *does not justify his opponents,* since their heavy, painstaking procedure is still less likely to bring to collection a horse who *cannot* be collected due to vertebral blockings. The German master Steinbrecht evokes horses who bump their knees as they are asked to perform a shoulder-in, and advises then for performing first a shoulder-in in a slimmer angle, and with more forward impulsion to avoid this from happening. This is very wise, but does not solve the problem in the least. It simply avoids it showing. Because as soon as the angle increases, the horse will bump his knees again, since no horsemanship, however careful and progressive, can take care of the vertebral blockings at the level of C7, T1, or T2, which hamper the proper movement of the shoulders (and in addition create pains in this area).

Now, briefly, what are these vertebral blockings, and how come they cannot be resolved spontaneously, or by means of "suppling" exercises like the shoulder-in?

They are programmed by the "brain" at large, that is, the intelligence which presides over the functioning of the nervous system, and correspond to a mechanism of safeguard. In a case of crisis (horse cast in his stall for instance), the brain sends a message of "spasm" to some small muscles fixed around the articular facets of a vertebra (or several vertebrae) in order to give more rigidity to a segment of the vertebral column, and therefore prevent further damage.

The snag is that when the crisis is over, the brain never sends any message of "end the alarm", and the reflex of defense becomes, in turn, a pathologic agent.

Programmed at the level of the "brain", these spasms can only be released by an order of the brain, resulting from a manipulation which will create a new "logic". These osteopathic manipulations are therefore different from the chiropractic manipulations, which address only the "mechanical", cosmetic aspect of the blocking, which the chiropractors call a "subluxation". Chiropractors' concern is the "alignment" of the vertebrae. Osteopaths' is their mobility.

Of course, osteopaths like Dr. Giniaux do not ignore that there are real subluxations at the level of "real" joints, like the elbow, the shoulder, the sacroiliac, and they will resolve these subluxations with the same type of manipulations as the chiropractors.

It is by necessity that I have evoked this difference between chiropractors and "osteopaths", in order to answer the questions that inevitably will arise in the reader's mind. All further development however would trespass the limits of this essay.

Appendix 2

This is an excerpt from the 12th Edition of the "METHOD."

English translation is mine.

Progression of the Training

Dismounted (work in hand)

Make the horse come toward the rider.[1]

Make the horse back up, his neck lifted, the rider holding with each hand the snaffle reins, with arms fully extended upwards (Fig. 16). The rider will start opposing the resistances of the weight and force through pulsated half-halts and repeated vibrations. Obtained through a force directed upwards, this elevated position of the neck forestalls "acculement" [2] (the horse's evading behind the bit) by transferring the weight backward within the limits of the backward movement.

One will make the horse back up only one step, keeping him as straight as possible from shoulders to haunches. One understands that the smallest deviation of the croup would hamper this precise transference of the weight: therefore great care should be taken asking for a second step only after the horse was replaced in a perfectly straight position, in order to avoid the resistances which would prevent him from understanding the intentions of the rider.

To this step by step reining back, where each step is followed with a momentary halt, allowing the cessation of any muscular contraction other than those necessary to the station, one will add working on two tracks, left and right, with reversed and direct pirouettes, taking care of asking only one step at a time, and halting the horse as soon as this step was made. The important point is that the parts which must be *momentarily immobilized do not move* (pirouettes) and that the transferences of weight follow the laws of balance and harmony in the movement. (Reining back and work on the haunches.)

One will then proceed to doing flexions, while insisting on the lateral flexion of the neck, with the snaffle first, then the curb; on the direct and semi-lateral flexion of the jaw, the rider facing the horse and lifting the head with the two reins of snaffle divided and held five inches from the rings, in order (important point) to make the jaw yield before the head. The same flexion will then be done with the curb, the rider holding a branch of the curb with each hand in order to lift the horse's head and get the same result.

The horse which has yielded to the more direct action of the snaffle may resist at first the action of the curb because of the curb chain being in the way; one will then come back to the snaffle, then to the curb until the horse, by yielding to this latter, shows that he understood the intentions of his master.

Remark. The lateral flexion of the neck destroyed all the resistances resulting from *retractions* or *contractures* of the neck muscles; the direct and semi-lateral flexions of the jaw, while withholding the neck and elevating the head, destroy the resistances that the jaw could offer in any position. This preparatory work will last four days, to familiarize the horse to the man, make him calm at the mounting, and make him understand the domination of the man.

But it is *on the back of the horse* that the rider will give him balance, that is, train him. This work in hand is not indispensable, but it is useful as a preparation, and this is why I recommend it for four days at the most. One should not sacrifice the principle to the accessory.

Troop horses may be worked in hand in this way for eight to ten days, during the first part of the lesson. This work in hand makes the obedience of the horse easier, establishes a confident relationship between him and his rider, who in turn, as he acknowledges the progress of his horse, becomes more indulgent and treats him in a kinder way.

On horseback

At a halt:

With the snaffle reins divided, lift the neck and give the reins only after the yielding of the jaw. Avoid the "acculement";[2] if resistances occur, use repeated half-halts and vibrations. *As a rule,* by the first lessons, the rider will use these new effects of the hand in order to destroy all the resistances of force or weight each time they will occur.

Repeat the lateral and semi-lateral flexions of the neck, as when working in hand. As soon as the rider has obtained a beginning of self-carriage of the neck and mobility of the jaw, he will set his horse in a walk and will work him right rein and left rein (if he is in an indoor arena) on straight and circular lines as well, seeking lightness and using the new effects of hand in order to destroy any resistance of weight or force, and avoiding any simultaneous use of the legs and the hand.

He will proceed on horseback as he did working in hand, i.e., he will walk one step or two, and will stop, giving with the hand only after obtainment of the mobility of the jaw, *release of the hand, and rest for the horse.* He then will gather the reins, ask once again for lightness and will bring the horse one or two steps forward, then stop again and follow the same gradation. He will alternate this work at a walk, so graduated, with backing ups, pirouettes, work on the haunches. The breaking down of each movement is so important and produces so extraordinary results, that I don't hesitate repeating myself and urging all the intelligent riders to follow exactly this gradation: 1) check if the horse is light or presents a resistance to the hand; 2) destroy this resistance through half-halts and vibrations, depending on its nature, get the mobility of the jaw and bring the horse one or two steps forward, while opposing immediately any resistance by using the new means, stop the horse and give the hand only after he is light, keep him calm, immobile at a halt for a half minute, and bring him again forward at a walk, after having checked the mobility of the jaw.

The like for backing up, reversed pirouettes and pirouettes, and two track work; ask only for one step, create again the position or lightness, and leave the horse alone, calm, resting for awhile, and go on following always the same gradation. These instants of rest, repeatedly asked for with this scrupulous attention, produce results which will surprise the rider. The muscular contraction ceases to be active, the horse feels good, reflects, and resumes his work without fatigue.

The new muscular contraction necessary to the locomotion profits by the relaxation which occurred during the resting period, and lends itself more readily to the harmony of forces, hence to balance, I mean to say, to the lightness of the horse. In addition, through such a graduated work, the rider imprints in the horse's mind the idea of the man's superiority and therefore assures his domination over his mount, all the while making his obeying easier.

To stop his horse, the rider will use first the "effets d'ensemble" (graduated opposition of hand and legs); but soon the hand will suffice to stop the horse straight from shoulders to haunches.

Since the combined action of legs and hand *immobilizes* the horse, one understands by the same token that when it is about a *movement* one should not use the same means.

The rider then will set his horse into a trot and will stop after a few strides, following the same gradation as in a walk; i.e., he will give him the *position* or lightness (mobility of the jaw) before setting out to trot; that, during these few strides of trot, he will fight the slightest resistances by using the new effects of hand, and that as he stops his horse he will ask one more time the mobility of the jaw, before leaving him at a rest, calm and immobile. He will continue for a few minutes the work at a trot, on straight and circular lines as well, following the same gradation as at a walk, that is, alternating rest and work in a more or less even proportion.

Then the rider will try on place (at a halt) to get some semblances of mobility of the extremities (limbs), in order to prepare the schooling for collection, and he will conclude the lesson with a few departures into canter, on both leads, *following always the same gradation* as in a trot or walk.

The rider will take care using his reins as I indicated in the chapter dealing with the new effects of reins, i.e., alternate the play of the snaffle and curb reins, in order to accustom his horse to keep *on his own* his balance and good position.

Here comes a very important observation:

Using the *direct rein* at a canter, right rein if the horse canters right lead, left rein if he canters left lead, in order to destroy the resistances through half-halts or vibrations, the rider gets at once a great lightness, keeps his horse straight, and makes the departures and hence the flying changes very easy.

All this work must be done without any fatigue for the horse, which the rider will teach by playing with him, by making him understand by the first that their conjugated efforts must tend to obtain the perfect equilibrium or the constant lightness: therefore he will ask from his horse the mellow mobility of the jaw before setting him into motion, and in this way will have made sure that the machine is ready to function. One understands the rapid progress which this gradation will provide in the education of the horse.

The teacher initiates by the first steps his pupil with all the difficulties he will have to meet underway, giving him the means to overcome them, and correcting immediately the slightest errors the horse may make by ignorance. Therefore two months of this rational education will have not passed before the intelligent rider enjoys results he would never have obtained, had he not given his horse the balance of the first genre or this perfect and constant lightness which allow the horse to execute with utmost easiness all the required movements, without the shadow of a resistance, and appreciating at once, or rather because he appreciates immediately, the slightest effects of the hand or the legs of the rider. The master demands, and the servant obeys.

When a horse, through all the principles taught in this last edition, has been brought to the balance of the first genre, all the resistances having disappeared, only soft means should be used. The hand will act through a slow, delicate, and minutely graduated force.

I have said what I believe to be the equestrian truth. I think it to be useful to the intelligent and serious riders to recommend them the progression I have just shown. I allow myself to give them a piece of advice from a friend, and I dare say, from an old friend, and tell them: discard my principles if they don't suit you; but if you acknowledge in them the equestrian truth, accept them as a whole, don't mutilate them, and remember that the author who has studied for forty years, knows enough the work of his whole life so as to appreciate the importance of all its parts.

[1] In the work in hand, Baucher would first teach his horses to come toward the rider when they were applied the whip on the chest. The rider would tap gently the horse's chest, every second or so, and pull the horse forward in the meantime. Progressively, the horse would relate the two facts, and then, move forward on his own as soon as the whip would touch his chest. In this way, Baucher would avoid any unasked for retrograde movement of the horse as he was working in hand.

[2] Acculement is a notion difficult to explain. The word bore different meanings in the French Tradition, depending on the times. La Guérinière equates it to "entablement", a drawback by which the horse, as he is working on two tracks, enlarges his hind track instead of narrowing it. This seems to correspond to a lack of proper engagement of the hind legs.

For Baucher on the contrary, "acculement" is when the horse goes too much on the haunches.

In his natural balance, a horse bears more weight on the front legs than on the rear legs. When correctly collected, the division of the weight becomes even. If then more weight is brought upon the rear legs, any movement is compromised, the forward movement as well as the rearward movement.